Notorious Women of Early California

Madams, Murderers, Schemers and Dreamers

Robin C. Johnson

California Venture Books

2022

Copyright© 2022 California Venture Books

All rights reserved. No part of this book may be reproduced or transmitted in any form or by any means, electronic or mechanical, including photocopying, without permission in writing from the publisher or author.

First Edition

Cover image courtesy of the California Archives.

Other Nonfiction Books by the Author

Fearless: Gutsy Gals of a Bygone Era

California Volcanoes: A Walking Guide

Geology Hikes of Northern California

Enchantress, Sorceress, Madwoman: The True Story of Sarah Althea Hill

Dedication

To women everywhere and throughout history who were bold enough to thwart convention and forge a singular life path.

Acknowledgements

The following agencies provided assistance and significant research materials and photographs for use in this book: The Bancroft Library at UC Berkeley and the California Archives.

I am deeply appreciative for the digitized newspaper collection of the University of California, Riverside, and the Chronicling America collection of the Library of Congress.

As always, I thank my partner, Dot Lofstrom, for her suggestions, criticisms, encouragement, and unflagging support.

CONTENTS

- INTRODUCTION 1
- I. MURDERERS 6
  - JOSEFA SEGOVIA (1825? – 1851) 7
  - LAURA FAIR (1837 – 1919) 11
  - CORDELIA BOTKIN (1856 – 1910) 18
  - EMMA LEDOUX (1875 – 1941) 25
- II. GAMBLERS AND THIEVES 36
  - ELEANOR DUMONT (1829 – 1879) 39
  - MABEL KEATING (1870 - ?) 48
  - JUANITA SPINELLI (1889 – 1941) 53
- III. HEIRESSES 62
  - LILLIE HITCHCOCK COIT (1843 - 1929) 63
  - AIMEE CROCKER (1863 – 1941) 69
- IV. GENDER BENDERS 81
  - CHARLEY PARKHURST (1812 – 1879) 86
  - JEANNE BONNET (1849 - 1876) 94
  - ELVIRA VIRGINIA MUGARRIETA (1869 – 1936) 101
- V. WOMEN OF ILL REPUTE 111
  - AH TOY (1828 – 1928?) 116
  - BELLE CORA (1832 - 1862) 121
  - JESSIE HAYMAN (1867 - 1923) 127
  - TESSIE WALL (1869 – 1932) 131
- VI. ADVENTURESSES 137
  - SARAH ALTHEA HILL (1850 – 1937) 140
  - MAUD NELSON (1865 – 1902) 154
  - VESTA HASTINGS (1866 – 1898) 161
- VII. PERFORMERS 168
  - LOLA MONTEZ (1821 - 1861) 171
  - DOLLY ADAMS (1860 – 1888) 188
  - ISADORA DUNCAN (1877 – 1927) 193
- ABOUT THE AUTHOR 206
- NOTES 207

INTRODUCTION

Until recently, recorded human history has primarily been an account of the activities of men. The few women who have had their names passed down to posterity fall roughly into three categories. There were those who were born or married into greatness—Marie Antoinette, Cleopatra, Queen Victoria. There were those who were great visionaries or achievers, contributing to the advancement of human progress as scientists, artists, and social reformers—Marie Curie, Jane Austen, Amelia Earhart, Harriet Tubman. Then there were those who achieved recognition for less savory reasons, for deeds that shocked, even horrified, their contemporaries—Lizzie Borden, Lady Godiva, Bonnie Parker. This last group is the subject of this book, the eccentric and scandalous women who achieved their celebrity in one of the most eccentric and scandalous of places—California during its first decades as an American state.

While Europeans had colonized and established a thriving society on the East Coast beginning in the seventeenth century, they had had little influence on the West Coast, which remained a great unknown to most of them. Before the 18th century, the only women on the Pacific Coast were Native Americans who had occupied this land for thousands of years. The first white men they encountered were Spanish explorers, Russian and French fur trappers, and a few adventurous mountain men like Kit Carson.

During the 18th century the Spanish began to slowly colonize the land they called Alta California. The Spanish soldiers who established their presidios at San Diego, Santa Barbara, Monterey, and San Francisco, took wives from the native populations. They then escorted missionaries who built a string of 21 missions along the El Camino Real, the King's Highway, between 1769 and 1821. In 1822 New Spain (Mexico) achieved its independence from Spain and obtained control of the territory.

The first settlers of European descent were men (almost exclusively) who obtained land grants (ranchos) from the Mexican government. One of these was Dr. John Marsh, who established a homestead at the base of Mount Diablo west of San Francisco. Because of conflicts with both Mexican authorities and Native Americans, he had trouble holding and operating his ranch. His solution was to start a campaign to draw other American settlers to California, hoping to increase the population to the point where the whites could wield some influence and help one another homestead in the western outback. Of course his description of California couldn't have been more rosy—vast swathes of untamed land, fertile and teeming with wildlife, practically free for any man willing to work it. That was true to an extent, but there were hardships to be endured that he failed to mention. There were no towns, no infrastructure, no reliable workforce, skirmishes with Native Americans, and corrupt Mexican bureaucrats who made business complicated. It was expensive and difficult to get supplies from the East, and overland travel without roads was nearly impossible. Only a few routes existed over the rugged Sierra Nevada mountains, and these were rough paths that posed serious risks to wagons.

Still, Marsh piqued the interest of a few families, and among those who first answered his call was the Bartleson-Bidwell Party from Missouri, led by John Bidwell, the founder of Chico, CA, and including Charles M. Weber, the founder of Stockton, CA. Nancy Kelsey (pictured) was a member of this party that traveled in wagons through Utah and Nevada, crossed the Sierra Nevada Mountains, and descended into Central California in 1841. She was 18 years old at the time and is considered to be the first white woman to set foot in California. She is also credited with sewing the first California flag, the Bear Flag, when the United States took the territory

Nancy Kelsey

during the Mexican-American War. As such, she has been given the nickname, "The Betsy Ross of California." She had several children, endured tremendous hardships, and survived attacks from bears and Native Americans. She was the mother of eight surviving children, was comfortable on horseback and with a rifle in her hand. She outlived most of the men who came out west with her, and maintained a hard-boiled and matter-of-fact attitude about all of it.

From Nancy Kelsey's arrival in California until 1900, California went from a bucolic wilderness with not a single paved road or bank to a major world destination boasting the sophisticated cities of San Francisco and Los Angeles, and a diverse population of citizens from around the globe. This accelerated development began in 1849 with the California Gold Rush.

When gold was discovered at Sutter's mill on the South Fork of the American River in 1848, everything changed with astonishing rapidity. The maritime gateway to the gold fields was through the San Francisco Bay, and people, mainly men, streamed in from everywhere. Between January 1848 and December 1849, the population of San Francisco burgeoned from 1,000 to 25,000.

The first half century of California's statehood must have been a deliciously exciting time and place to be. It was barbarous, bawdy, international, fast-paced, an in-your-face antidote to the long civilized East Coast. It made millionaires by the dozens and ruined men and women by the thousands. But, above all, it was a place where people from all over the world came with their dreams, as they had originally come to America itself.

Vast hordes of rowdy, fortune-seeking men poured into the state, forcing a swift build-up of infrastructure. Women came too, although in lesser numbers and at a slower pace. Some came as wives of businessmen. Some came as entrepreneurs, providing much-needed entertainment, lodging, laundries, restaurants and, of course, brothels. There was opportunity in the new territory, and so many more and surer ways to make a fortune than gold mining. Other women came for varying personal reasons. Such a one was the author, reformer, and abolitionist Eliza Farnham who came to San Francisco in 1849 to see to her deceased husband's affairs. After being carried over the mud flats from her ship and placed ashore, she realized what a novelty a woman was in the new world. "At that period in the history of San Francisco," she wrote, "it was so rare to see a female, that those whose misfortune it was to be obliged to be abroad felt themselves uncomfortably stared at. Doorways filled instantly, and little islands in the streets were thronged with men who seemed to gather in a moment, and who remained immovable till the spectacle passed from their incredulous gaze."[1]

Many women found that their scarcity in California was their advantage. That was particularly true for prostitutes and their madams who flourished in the new state. For these entrepreneurs, the lack of women wasn't the only advantage. Lack of law and order served them just as well. Towns sprang up overnight with makeshift jails and instant and shifting lawmen, and cities saw so many transient visitors that keeping the peace was impossible. There was vigilante justice, lynchings by self-righteous mobs, and plenty of impromptu killings over the slightest offense. Even in the courtrooms that did exist, gunshots were not uncommon.

From this strange, artificially accelerated beginning, California inherited a unique cultural identity characterized by diversity, daring, and innovation, the effects of which can be felt even into modern times. The women who helped shape California were likewise pioneers, and some of them were as eccentric as California itself.

The women in this book are not the Nancy Kelseys and Eliza Farnhams of early California. They are instead the women whose reputations were gained not from good works but from outrageous living.

They span a wide range of types and occupations, but they all have one thing in common—they were bold and unique. They were free spirits with little regard for convention or public opinion, often leaving society at large openmouthed. Some were truly bad actors, murderers and thieves, but they were not all bad in the sense of law breaking. In fact, some contributed much value to society. Still, they all broke the rules by which most people lived and by doing so became larger than life. The vast majority of people who didn't break the rules, it's worth noting, have been thoroughly forgotten.

The stories that follow continue to intrigue and fascinate us to this day. For better or worse, these women remain an unforgettable part of the colorful tableau of California history and will no doubt live on in infamy for centuries to come.

I. MURDERERS

Throughout history, murder has primarily been the domain of men, so much so that when a woman kills someone, people become morbidly fascinated with the crime. During the 1800s, the method of choice for female murderers was poison, the hands-down favorite being arsenic. Arsenic was cheap and easily obtained at that time, as it was commonly used for a variety of household purposes, such as poisoning rats.

A nineteenth-century woman defendant charged with a violent crime was less likely to be convicted and imprisoned than a man charged with the same crime. Victorian sensibilities made it difficult for men to blame women for such crimes or to ascribe cold-blooded calculation to them, preferring to think that violent women were victims of insanity or hysteria, and therefore not responsible for their actions. The other problem men had convicting women of murder was the possibility of capital punishment, and the idea of putting a woman to death was unthinkable to many. As a result of these attitudes, few women accused of murder were punished with the severity of their male counterparts, and many women literally got away with murder.

The exceptions in early California were women of color. There were large populations of Native Americans and Mexicans in the territory, many of whom were residents before the influx of white men during the Gold Rush. White immigrants brought their prejudices with them, and after taking the territory from the Mexicans in 1848, they dispensed justice more harshly on people of color than they did on their own kind. This was true even for accused females. The most glaring example may be that of Josefa Segovia, a Mexican American woman accused of murder. Her sad story kicks off this chapter.

I. MURDERERS

JOSEFA SEGOVIA (1825? – 1851)
"Juanita, the Mexican woman"

(From William Downie's *Hunting for Gold*, 1893)

The story of Josefa Segovia is surrounded by legend and mystery. There are a handful of written accounts made either by eye witnesses or by friends and relatives of eye witnesses and a couple of brief newspaper stories to inform us of the facts. Of course, like many historical events, even the eye witness accounts vary in many details. But where they mainly agree, we can reliably reconstruct the tragic day in a Gold Rush town that left two people dead.

It was 1851 in Downieville, California, a small mining town located on the North Fork of the Yuba River. The town was merely a collection of tents, cabins, and a handful of public buildings, mostly saloons. It served as a destination for miners in surrounding camps throughout Sierra County. That was especially true on the Fourth of July, only the second such celebration in the state's history, during which thousands of men flooded the town to watch a parade, listen to speeches, and to go on a day-long drinking binge, overcrowding the saloons and pouring out into the streets until the wee hours of the morning.

One of the revelers was a massive Scotsman named Joe (or Jack or Frederick) Cannon. He was affable and well liked, a popular fellow around town who on this day drank himself into a boisterous state of rowdiness during which he and his buddies roared down the streets banging on doors and whooping it up.

One of the doors on Cannon's route was that of Josefa Segovia, a young Mexican woman who lived with her lover (or husband), gambler José Loaiza, in a modest adobe on the main street of town. Josefa was about twenty-six years old, just five feet tall, slender, and beautiful. She and José had come from Mexico, along with throngs of their countrymen, following the lure of gold. It is estimated that between 1848 and 1852 as many as 25,000 Mexicans migrated to California to mine. But Josefa was one of very few women in town. Due to her beauty and the rarity of her sex, she was familiar to everyone.

The details of what happened when Cannon arrived at Josefa's house vary from one account to another, leaving both his intentions and actions subject to speculation. At any rate, he crashed into the house in a boisterous manner and accosted the young woman, terrifying and offending her. Cannon soon staggered back into the street with his friends and went on his way, leaving Josefa rattled but unharmed.

The following day, sobered up, he went back to the house, ostensibly to apologize. He spoke with a limited Spanish vocabulary and an unknown amount of sincerity. Whatever transpired between them enraged Josefa. She picked up a knife and stabbed him through the heart, killing him on the spot.

As soon as the news got out, an angry mob descended on her home, taking her away for a quick trial with a jury manned by Cannon's friends. There were a couple of people in town who attempted to come to Josefa's aid, but the mob shouted them down and threatened violence against any man who tried to help her.

At the trial, Dr. Cyrus D. Aiken, who had examined Josefa, testified that she was pregnant and therefore could not be hanged. The court ordered her to be examined by others present who had no medical training. They returned to say that Aiken had lied, that Josefa was not pregnant.

The prosecution painted Josefa as an angry and violent person, saying she stabbed Cannon without provocation. The defense was nonexistent.

She was quickly found guilty and sentenced to hang that afternoon. A scaffold was built on the Yuba River bridge and a man known as Big Logan was appointed hangman. Josefa was led through town to the scaffold. Dressed in her best clothes and a straw hat, her hair neatly braided, she walked through the jeering crowd with an air of defiance, showing no fear while they pounded the air with fists and shouted, "A life for a life!" Men numbering about 500 lined the banks of the river to witness the event. Once upon the platform Josefa called to the throng that she had no regrets, and that if she were provoked like that again, she would do the same.

Big Logan stood beside her, the noose in his hand, hesitant to hang a woman. Josefa tossed her hat to a friend, then took the rope from the hangman and put the noose around her own neck, pulling up her hair to free it from the rope. She tightened the noose, called out, "Adiós Señores!" then leapt from the scaffold into eternity.

The following day Josefa and Cannon were buried beside one another on a nearby hillside.

On July 14, 1851, nine days after the hanging, the *Daily Alta California* had the following to say: "The violent proceedings of an indignant and excited mob led on by the enemies of the unfortunate woman are a blot upon the history of the state. Had she committed a crime of really heinous character, a real American would have revolted at such a course as was pursued toward this friendless and unprotected foreigner...The perpetrators of the deed have shamed themselves and their race. The Mexican woman is said to have borne herself with the utmost fortitude and composure through the fearful ordeal, meeting her fate without flinching." Modern historians agree that if Josefa had been white, she would not have been lynched. Newspapers would also have used her name rather than referring to her as "the Mexican woman." The *Alta* got the story from the deputy sheriff of Downieville.

Did he even know her name? Down through the ages, the name given to her was Juanita (a generic Mexican name) by those wishing to give her back her humanity. Later scholars were able to unearth her actual name.

Josefa was the first woman executed in California. A plaque titled "In Memory of Juanita," and containing an abbreviated version of her story, was placed on the Craycroft Building in Downieville by the Major William Downie chapter of E Clampus Vitus in 1996, memorializing a dark chapter in early California history.

LAURA FAIR (1837 – 1919)
"The Woman in Black"

Laura Fair (University of Nevada, Reno)

By the age of 28, the tall, regal, blue-eyed Laura had already been married four times and had a reputation as a woman who should not be trifled with. She was no shrinking violet. She was bold, flirtatious, and impudent. Unfortunately for the philandering attorney Alexander P. Crittenden, Laura did not come with a warning label.

Born in Mississippi in 1837, Laura Lane married for the first time at age sixteen. Her first husband died of cholera soon after and Laura married again. She left that husband after a year, citing his continuous drunkenness as the reason. In 1856 nineteen year old Laura came to California to join her mother, who ran a boarding house in San Francisco. To earn a living, Laura taught music until 1859 when she married lawyer Colonel William D. Fair, a prominent citizen and early settler of Stockton, California. She thought she was set for life at that point, but Fair's law firm was foundering. He moved the family to San Francisco, hoping for a turn of fortune. The couple soon had a child, daughter Lillian. In 1861, when their daughter was one and a half years old, the distraught Colonel Fair fatally shot himself. The cause of his despair is often blamed on Laura because she had cheated on him, but the facts remain unclear. At any rate, his legal practice was a failure, and he had barely been able to support his family. Twenty-four year old Laura was left with nothing.

Alone in the world, she turned to acting, and by 1863 had earned enough money to buy the 37-room Tahoe House hotel in Virginia City, Nevada, a town in the center of the Nevada silver boom. A transplanted Southerner living in a Union state during the Civil War, Laura was a secessionist. She shot a man because he tried to raise an American flag over her hotel. The man was wounded, but recovered, and Laura was acquitted.

Traveling between Nevada City and San Francisco was a steady stream of lawyers and bankers opening up new branches in Nevada to service the mining industry. One of these lawyers was Alexander P. Crittenden, handsome, distinguished, and twenty years older than Laura. The two quickly became lovers. Crittenden had a wife, Clara, and six children, but he made no attempt to hide his affair or spare his wife's feelings. When Laura moved back to San Francisco in 1866, they lived together and went around town together as a couple. Clara Crittenden knew about her husband's mistress, but she refused to divorce him.

The affair was tempestuous from the start, having at its core the impediment of the Crittenden marriage. Laura pressed Alex to divorce his wife and marry her. He resisted, giving her hope one day and despair the next as the years dragged on. They quarreled frequently and broke up just as often, always over the same issue, that he was not free to marry her. Once Laura fired her gun at Crittenden on the stairs to his office. She missed him and he shrugged it off. However, after one rocky period between them, Crittenden returned to Clara, and Laura's hopes of ever becoming his wife vanished. She met a handsome young man named Jesse Snyder and married him in August 1869.

It was now Crittenden's turn to feel betrayed. The loss of Laura to another man drove him straight back to her with renewed ardor. He demanded she leave Snyder and return to him, making renewed vows of love and promises that he was finally and utterly done with his wife. After only two months of marriage, Laura divorced Snyder, leaving his head spinning. He left San Francisco and went back home, convinced that the Wild West was far too wild for him.

In early November 1870 the affair between Laura Fair and Alex Crittenden reached a critical moment. Clara had been absent for several months, visiting relatives on the east coast with two of her children. On the night before their return, Laura and Crittenden discussed the matter at length and agreed that this time things would be different. Laura told him he must be brutally heartless to Clara, turning a cold eye and shoulder in her direction at all times.

Over the years of their stormy relationship, both of these lovers had threatened to kill themselves if either should leave, and Crittenden confided in friends that he was afraid Laura was fully capable of taking her own life. On the occasion of his wife's return, he most certainly was thinking of this possibility. He promised to make his wife understand that he had no affection left for her and their marriage was over. In the face of his stony behavior, he said, she would lose all hope and agree to a divorce. Soon, he assured Laura, the two of them would be married and be forever together.

It should be no surprise that by now Laura no longer trusted her lover's promises. On November 3, 1870, she dressed head to toe in her favorite color, black, including a black veil, and secretly followed him to Oakland where he was to escort his family aboard the El Capitan ferry for the last leg of their homeward journey. Laura boarded the ferry and stood in an unobtrusive place where she could watch the other passengers board. Crittenden, his wife, his son and his daughter came aboard the boat and sat together, Crittenden between his wife and daughter, an arm around each, chatting amiably, acting the perfectly dutiful and affectionate husband and father.

Laura grew enraged at the sight. He had betrayed her again! Just as the vessel pulled away from the dock, she emerged from the shadows and marched over to the family. She cried, "You've been the ruin of both me and my daughter!" Then she pulled out a Sharp's derringer and shot him point blank in the chest. She dropped the gun and fled to another part of the boat.

Crittenden slumped over onto his wife and she cradled his head in her lap until a doctor rushed in to administer stimulants. When the ferry reached San Francisco, the unconscious man was loaded into a carriage and taken to his house where surgeons removed the bullet.

Meanwhile, when the boat docked, Laura was taken to jail where she became hysterical, screaming and raving about Crittenden, her daughter and her mother. Alarmingly, she even took a bite out of a water glass. The next day she was still distracted, talking continuously and incoherently, moaning and crying. By the time Crittenden died after forty-eight hours of agony, Laura had quieted down and become calm.

Laura Fair went on trial in 1871 at the age of thirty-three. Witnesses from the ferry described her as "the woman in black," and the nickname stuck. The courtroom was packed every day for the month-long trial. Among those in attendance were women's rights leaders Susan B. Anthony and Elizabeth Cady Stanton who were sympathetic to the defendant. The prosecution painted Laura as a fallen woman and a seductress who had preyed on the hapless Crittenden while Laura's

I. MURDERERS

attorneys mounted a novel defense. The doctors brought in to testify, including her own personal doctor, claimed she shot Crittenden during a fit of temporary insanity brought on by insomnia and "retarded menstruation," which in modern times would be analogous to pre-menstrual syndrome. Temporary insanity was first used as a defense in 1859 and was extremely unusual at the time. Laura was described as a nervous, hysteria-prone personality, especially around the time right before menstruation. Her lawyers may have thought the gentlemen of the jury could appreciate this condition. But they did not.

Laura was found guilty of premeditated murder and sentenced to hang. When the verdict was announced, she sat in her chair unmoved, "like marble."

Although the male jury was satisfied with Laura's punishment, many females were not. It was Crittenden who had led Laura astray, they claimed, forcing her to live in sin by his refusal to divorce his wife. After years of broken promises and cruel emotional abuse, it was no surprise, they said, that Mrs. Fair went berserk. The lying adulterer deserved what he got! Emily Pitts Stevens, founder of the California Woman Suffrage Association, wrote, "Hang this woman, and the very name of San Francisco will be odious for ages to come!"

Laura Fair remained in prison while her appeal was filed. Her daughter Lillian, now fourteen, visited often. Her request for a retrial was granted on technicalities, one of those being that the question of her morals and chastity, a gross impropriety, were discussed during the first trial.

On October 1, 1872, nearly two years after the murder of Crittenden, the second jury found her not guilty by reason of insanity. Nearly all of the jurors genuinely believed that she had been hysterical at the time of the murder and for a few days afterward, so crazed by her hormonal imbalances that she didn't know what she was doing and should not be held accountable. For one holdout juror, a gallon of whisky provided during deliberations, helped him understand the facts. The following day, a representative from the Commission of Lunacy arrived to examine her and was hard pressed to find any evidence of lingering insanity, so Laura was freed.

There was outrage across the land at what was termed a mockery of justice. "A marvelously ignorant San Francisco jury," said the *New York Times*, "has given the extraordinary verdict of acquittal which turns loose upon society a woman who has outraged nearly all the fundamental principles on which society rests." Laura was vilified in the press by those who had never laid eyes on her and had no firsthand knowledge of the case. But temporary insanity as a defense for murder was considered a legal con by many. This was true, actually, well into the twentieth century.

Laura Fair then launched herself onto the lecture circuit to clear her reputation and raise money to pay her legal debts. Women were admitted to her talks for free, but men had to pay a dollar. She lectured on and off throughout the 1870s on a country-wide circuit, retelling her story and decrying the press and pulpit of San Francisco. "The woman in San Francisco," she claimed during her New York tour, "who has not some scandal sticking to her skirts is as hard to find as a white blackbird or an honest New York politician."

One of many people captivated by the case, Mark Twain incorporated it into his first published novel, *The Gilded Age: A Tale of To-Day* (1873).

Despite Laura's notoriety in San Francisco, she remained in the city and settled down to a quiet life with her mother and daughter. The outrage that had erupted at the time of the trial soon faded and was ultimately replaced with a fond sense of ownership by San Franciscans, the sort of attitude that normally manifests itself long after the subject is gone. Far from being ostracized for her crime, Laura became a local celebrity, was often invited to chic parties, and enjoyed the attention of society and the press as if she were royalty.

Her daughter also suffered no stigma from her mother's crime. In

Lillian Lorraine Hollis

1892 Lillian was voted the most beautiful girl on the Pacific Coast in a newspaper-sponsored contest. She became an actress and went by the stage name Lillian Lorraine Hollis. She left San Francisco for New York and became estranged from her mother. She was quite successful as an actress and Ziegfeld girl from 1909 to 1912. She then starred in several short films. Later she started her own stock company and managed actors, wrote plays, and published a novelette.

But both shame and fame eventually faded away, and Laura was left impoverished and alone. With no more traction to be gained from her notoriety, she went by her actual legal name of Laura Snyder. In 1906 she moved across the bay to more affordable Richmond, renting a room in a humble home where she made a few dollars doing odd jobs like babysitting. At the age of seventy, she was still described as beautiful.

In 1913 Laura was shocked to read in a newspaper of the death of her daughter. Lillian had fallen on hard times and died of starvation in a squalid room on West Forty-ninth Street, leaving behind several orphaned cats. Laura became hysterical, brandishing a butcher knife and threatening to kill herself. She was restrained and taken to the hospital for observation.

Laura herself passed away in 1919 of heart failure at the age of 82, her claim to fame as a murderess long forgotten by her contemporaries. But her story has been resurrected for current and future generations and is now a renowned episode in San Francisco's vibrant criminal history.

CORDELIA BOTKIN (1856 – 1910)
"Candy Box Poisoner"

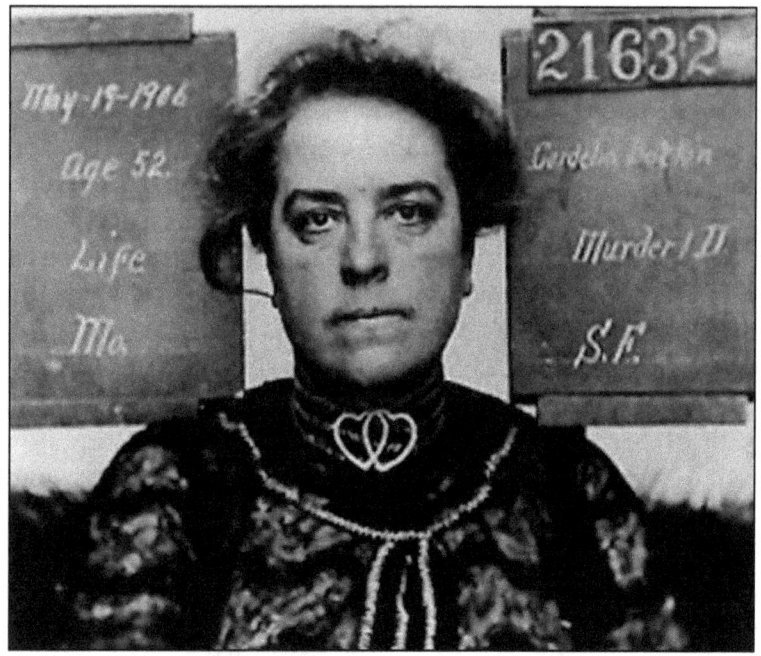

Cordelia Botkin (Delaware Archives)

Forty-year-old Cordelia Adelaide Botkin sat on a bench in San Francisco's Golden Gate Park chatting with a friend when a young man riding by on a bicycle broke down. As he fixed his bike, he introduced himself to the women, then sat down beside them and joined their conversation. He was thirty-three-year-old John Preston Dunning, superintendent of the Associated Press's Western Division. He was married and the father of a baby daughter. That chance meeting would spell doom for both Botkin and Dunning, as well as several others.

Cordelia was an unlikely femme fatale. She was middle aged, short, stout with dark brown hair, and she spoke with a fake English accent designed to give herself airs. She had been born in Missouri in 1856 and had never set foot in England. Like Dunning, she too was married, to Welcome A. Botkin, a salesman for Armour meats. The Botkins had moved from

I. MURDERERS

Missouri to Stockton, California, where they had raised their only child, son Beverly. Once their son was an adult, Cordelia and Welcome informally separated because of, in Cordelia's words, "diverse temperaments." Cordelia moved to San Francisco where she did as she pleased, supported by a monthly allowance from her husband. She had rooms in a boarding house on Geary Street, which is where, after their meeting in the park, John Dunning began to show up with regularity.

Dunning had a weakness for alcohol and gambling, losing money at the horse races on a regular basis. With Cordelia at his side, his bad habits only got worse. He was often drunk, often broke. His wife, Mary Elizabeth, finally gave up trying to reform him and in 1896 left for Dover, Delaware, to live with her parents.

Freed from any concern about his family, Dunning took rooms at the same boarding house as Cordelia, and they spent their nights in revelry, drinking and playing cards with Cordelia's best friend, Louise Seeley, a pretty blonde widow from Chicago. Sometimes Cordelia's son Beverly would join them at cards.

The landlady described the group as "too lively," and she had to intervene on more than one occasion to tell them to quiet down due to complaints from the other tenants. One evening, for instance, Louise was entertaining herself by jumping off Beverly's shoulders onto the floor and the boarder beneath complained that he was afraid the chandelier was going to come crashing down on top of him.

Dunning's gambling debts grew to such an unmanageable amount that he embezzled $4,000 from AP office funds. When his crime was discovered, he was fired. Cordelia, with her husband's money, helped him as much as she was able, but Dunning was growing more and more depressed over being unemployed, as well as feeling guilty for abandoning his wife and baby.

In the spring of 1898 the Spanish-American war broke out, and the Associated Press offered Dunning a position as a war correspondent. He had a track record as an excellent field reporter, having worked on assignments in Samoa and Chile before being promoted to management at the Associated Press. He decided to accept the offer and go off to the war. Although he had apparently had enough of the fast life with Cordelia, she hadn't had enough of him. She pleaded with him to stay with her, but off he went to Cuba where he helped save survivors from the Spanish ships that were sunk in the Battle of Santiago de Cuba on July 2, 1898. In desperation, Cordelia wrote a letter to the governor, asking to be posted to Cuba as a nurse. She received no answer.

Meanwhile, Dunning wrote letters to both his lover and his wife, letting them both understand that he wished to reform and return to his family.

Cordelia realized she had to do something to prevent that happy reunion. She wrote anonymous letters to Mary Dunning, telling her that her husband was still cheating on her and warning her not to take him back, signing the letters, "A Friend."

But separation had been good for the Dunnings and they began to heal their relationship and make plans for the future. He lined up a job with a New York newspaper for after the war. Cordelia grew frantic.

On a visit to Stockton to visit her friend Elmira Ruoff, Cordelia pelted her with questions about poison, in particular arsenic, implying that she might poison herself. She asked where one could buy it and how much it might take to kill somebody. She then claimed to be ill and called a doctor. She asked the doctor the same troubling questions.

Dunning continued to write to both women from Cuba and then from Puerto Rico, trying to ease himself out of Cordelia's life. He told her he would not be returning to California after the war, but would reunite with his wife in Delaware. Ignoring all evidence to the contrary, Cordelia was convinced that Dunning still loved her, if only she could find a way to keep him from returning to his wife.

On August 9, 1898, a package from San Francisco addressed to Mary Dunning arrived at the Pennington home in Delaware. Inside was a one-pound box of chocolates wrapped in a lace handkerchief, containing a note that read, "With love to yourself and baby. Mrs. C." Ah, dear Mrs. Corbaley, Mary thought, picturing her old friend back in San Francisco. Had she any reason to be suspicious of the gift, she might have seen, upon careful examination, that some of the bonbons had surface cracks in them where someone had opened them, inserted something, then carefully reshaped the rupture. But Mary had no such suspicions, especially since the package appeared to be from a trusted friend.

After a dinner of trout and corn fritters, the family retired to the front porch to chat with the neighbors and Mary brought out the candy to share. Her parents declined, but Mary, her sister, niece, nephew Harry and the neighbors, Miss Josephine Bateman and Miss Ethel Millington, indulged their chocolate cravings.

Several hours later, after everybody had gone to bed, Mary's sister Ida Deane began to vomit. One by one, all six candy eaters got violently ill. John Pennington, Mary's father, called a doctor. He diagnosed them with cholera morbus, a condition associated with improperly refrigerated food. The doctor pointed to the corn fritters as the likely cause. But the two sick neighbors had not eaten dinner with the rest of the family, a fact that nobody noticed at the time. Eventually, everyone recovered except Mary and her sister. They got worse. Their father called in another doctor who concluded that they had been poisoned. By now they knew the candy was to blame but it was too late to prevent a tragedy. The two sisters died and the story erupted across the country. It was the first time in American history that the U.S. Mail had been used for murder.

John Pennington had three pieces of the uneaten candy tested for poison. The chemist found a substantial amount of arsenic. One piece of the arsenic, he said, was as large as a pea, and he added that there was enough of the poison in the three pieces of candy to kill four people.

When John Dunning received a telegram from his father-in-law informing him of his wife's death, he rushed from Puerto Rico to Delaware and was confronted by the "A Friend" letters and the note that had come with the candy. He immediately recognized the handwriting as that of Cordelia Botkin and told the police of his suspicions.

As the news broke that Mrs. Botkin was a suspect in this shocking case, Cordelia left her sister's home in Healdsburg and fled to Stockton to be protected by her husband. She tried to go into seclusion, staying at one hotel then another to avoid reporters. Welcome Botkin faced the press to defend his wife. "I know my wife is innocent of any crime or any wrong doing," he insisted. "She is incapable of committing the atrocious murder of two innocent women, neither of whom she knew." [2]

Cordelia again visited her friend Mrs. Ruoff, who asked Cordelia if she remembered their earlier visit with all the talk of poison. Cordelia shot back, "You put all those thoughts in my head!" She then fell onto the floor and became hysterical.

On August 22 Cordelia agreed to speak to a reporter from San Francisco's *The Call* in her rooms at the Windsor Hotel, where she sat fanning herself nervously during the interview. She emphatically denied any connection with the "awful, fiendish double murder." She also denied that she and Dunning were anything but dear friends, that she had no interest in him romantically and wouldn't have married him even if he were single. Everything being said about her, she claimed, was vicious slander.

"Mr. Dunning idolized his wife and darling little girl," she told the reporter, "and his despair was most pitiable when they left him and went East. He often said, 'It would be far better for them if I were dead.' He carried a life insurance of $12,500 and often went without food to meet the premiums so his family would be provided for after his death."[3]

She went on to paint a picture of herself as a saint. "The publication of every act of my life would not bring a blush to my brow or cause my husband, son or sister to feel the slightest sense of shame."

Two days after this interview, Cordelia opened the door to two policemen. She submitted calmly to her arrest as Mrs. Ruoff and her husband looked on.

"I feel quite calm now," she said in a statement to the *Call*. "The excitement and shocks of the past few days are no more." Turning to her husband, whom she addressed as "Pop," she asked that he send for her son Beverly. A reporter went on this mission and found the young man in the saloon with a friend. When told of his mother's arrest and desire to see him he waved the matter aside as not deserving his attention. "He has taken the developments of the past few days much to heart," said the reporter, "and the drunken condition in which he was found this evening was his normal condition of the last few days." [4]

Cordelia was taken to the County Jail where her husband caressed her hand and she reassured him over and over that everything would be all right.

The investigation that followed made it clear that Cordelia had not made much effort to cover her tracks. The candy was traced to the George Haas confectionary in San Francisco, but no one could positively say Cordelia had been in the store. A clerk at the Owl Drug store in San Francisco identified Cordelia as having bought arsenic from him, and the lace handkerchief that had accompanied the box of candy was traced to the City of Paris department store. The clerk who had sold the handkerchief confidently identified Cordelia as the buyer. A handwriting analyst conclusively matched Cordelia's handwriting to the letters and the note. A witness, John Fennessee, came forward to say that he had seen a nervous acting Cordelia on August 4 at the ferry post office, putting a candy box sized package in the parcel drop at 5:55 p.m.

In December 1898 Cordelia was tried on two counts of first degree murder, Judge Carroll Cook presiding. After deliberating for four hours, the jury found her guilty, and she was sentenced to life in prison. Judge Cook lamented that he was unable to send her to the gallows, since the jury had removed that option.

Cordelia was held at the County Jail to wait for her appeal. The following year her husband filed for divorce. In 1901 the state Supreme Court granted Cordelia a new trial. A year later, still in jail, she told people she was certain she would soon be free. Her plan for her next chapter was to become an actress. But the wheels of justice turned excruciatingly slow. In 1904 Welcome Botkin died. The following year their son Beverly died. Cordelia was escorted from the jail to view his body.

She finally had a second trial in 1904 and was again found guilty and sentenced to life in prison. She appealed that decision after the Great Fire of 1906, in which some of the evidence against her was destroyed, but the appeal was denied.

In 1906 Cordelia asked to be moved from the overcrowded County Jail, hoping to get roomier digs. Her request was granted and she was transferred to San Quentin Prison where she remained until her death, perpetually maintaining her innocence in the poisoned candy murder.

John Dunning died of a cerebral hematoma in Philadelphia in 1907, a ruined man, whose drinking had left him unemployed and financially destitute.

Cordelia died at the age of 56 on March 7, 1910. The official cause of death was "softening of the brain due to melancholy." She was buried in Oak Mound Cemetery in Healdsburg, California.

Although Cordelia Botkin's method of delivering poison to her victim was an unusual one, poisoning by arsenic in the 19th century was all the rage. Arsenic was cheap and easy to get, it was odorless and colorless, and was the most common poison used to remove troublemakers, especially by women. But sending poison (or anything deadly) through the mail is a sloppy approach to murder. There are so many ways the deed can go wrong. In this case, the poison did hit its mark, but, then, it also killed an unintended victim. That detail did not seem to cause Cordelia much remorse.

EMMA LEDOUX (1875 – 1941)
"The Trunk Murderess"

Emma LeDoux's mug shot (California Archives)

There were two big national news stories coming out of California in 1906. The biggest was the April 18 earthquake (historically known as The Great Earthquake) and subsequent fire that destroyed most of San Francisco. The other was the arrest of Emma LeDoux on March 26 for the premeditated murder of her husband, Albert N. McVicar. Both were sensational stories at the time, though the latter eventually faded from public consciousness so that very few people today have heard of Emma LeDoux, the notorious trunk murderess.

Emma Theresa Cole was born in Pine Grove, California, on September 10, 1875, to parents Thomas Jefferson Cole and native Californian Mary Ann Runyon Cole. Emma was the eldest of eight children, mostly girls. The family moved to a farm in Cold Spring Canyon, Oregon, when she was a toddler. After her father died, Mary Ann moved the family back to Amador County, California. She married English miner James Head in 1886 when Emma was eleven years old.

Emma married her first husband, Charles A. Barrett, in 1892 at the age of sixteen with her mother's consent. She divorced him in 1898 and married a Cornish miner named William Stanley Williams three years later. They were married in Reno, Nevada, then moved to Arizona where Williams worked a mine near the town of Globe. A victim of consumption, Williams had been sickly throughout his short marriage. He died suddenly of gastroenteritis in June 1902, leaving Emma well provided for through a $10,000 life insurance policy.

Not one to stay single long, two months later Emma married Albert McVicar in Bisbee, Arizona. The two returned to California, but marital bliss did not last long. McVicar went through Emma's $10,000 windfall in no time, investing in a retail business in San Francisco that failed. He then urged her into prostitution and the two of them lived off her earnings, both of them feeding a destructive morphine addiction. Eventually, McVicar left Emma and went to work as a timber man for the Rawhide Mine in Jamestown, California, divorcing her soon after. Single again, Emma moved back to Amador County to live with her mother at her Jackson ranch.

She then went on a dating spree, enjoying her freedom. She dated her childhood sweetheart, Frenchman Eugene LeDoux, as well as Joseph Healy, a plumber in San Francisco, ending up engaged to them both. LeDoux won out and the two were married in August 1905 just before Emma turned 30. LeDoux, it turned out, was an alcoholic who went on week-long drinking binges. Still, Emma was determined to make this marriage work, as she had already had her share of disruption and disappointment.

After a two-year separation from his wife, McVicar began to miss her. He wrote to her and her mother saying that he wanted her back. When he learned that she was remarried, he threatened to bring bigamy charges and ruin her marriage to LeDoux. Although she and McVicar were actually divorced, there are many reasons that she would have been alarmed at his reappearance and his threats. Her multiple marriages on top of a divorce, a rarity in those days, would have been seen as shameful, but even more scandalous was the lifestyle she had lived during her marriage to McVicar. The last thing she would have wanted was for him to turn up and start blabbing. Clearly, she had to make sure that didn't happen.

She invited him to join her in San Francisco. Happy to think his ex-wife wanted to get back together, he met her on March 10, 1906, and the two of them lived the high life for several days. On March 15 they went out to dinner, indulging in oysters and champagne, and later that evening, McVicar got deathly ill. Emma called a doctor she knew, Dr. Dillon, who treated her husband for food poisoning. While he was there, she asked him for morphine to help her sleep, and he gave it to her. Two days later she went to his office and asked for two ounces of cyanide of potassium to develop some photographs. Suspecting nothing, the doctor gave her the order for the drug store. She filled it at the Baldwin Pharmacy. Meanwhile, McVicar lay in bed at the hotel, gradually recovering.

Emma was thinking ahead, trying to make sure that McVicar wouldn't be missed, at least not for a while. She knew he had no relatives nearby, that the closest was a brother in Colorado whom she had never met. His job at the mine was a problem, however. She told McVicar she wanted him to come live with her on the ranch and persuaded him to give up his job. He quit on March 21 and took $163 in wages that he was due. The couple used most of this money on a furniture shopping trip at the Stockton Bruener's store, putting $100 down on their $127.50 purchase. They then went out to dinner and drinks, then retired to their room at Stockton's California Hotel where McVicar dreamily imagined a night of connubial bliss. But Emma had other plans. Instead of canoodling, she gave him an elephant sized dose of morphine.

The following morning, March 24, her husband unconscious on the bed, she called Bruener's and had them change the delivery address of McVicar's furniture from his home to the residence of new husband Eugene LeDoux in Jackson. She then went out to Rosenbaum & Co. and bought the largest trunk they had, four feet long, which was shorter than she'd hoped, and had it delivered to her room. Next she went to H. C. Shaw's hardware store and bought rope and was back to her room in time to accept the trunk delivery. She managed to stuff the 200-pound McVicar, who was still alive, into the trunk, using his clothing as packing, then she called for a hotel employee to tie it up with the rope and take it to the train station. The boy who came for the trunk couldn't manage it alone, as it was too heavy, so he called for help and the two men loaded it on a wagon.

While waiting for her train's departure time, Emma went shopping and bought a new hat. When she arrived at Stockton's Southern Pacific depot, she was irritated to find that the trunk had not yet been delivered. For the first time that day, she got agitated. She waited impatiently for the trunk, continually checking the clock. She was about to call the hotel when the trunk finally arrived. Although the train had not yet left for Jackson, she was told that it was too late to load it. Cool-headed Emma's anxiety level spiked. She watched the train leave the station without her and, more importantly, without the trunk, which stood beside her, looming massively.

Her plan had been to take the trunk to her Amador County ranch where the body would have been easy to dispose of. Nobody would even notice that McVicar wasn't around. If his distant relatives ever thought to ask after him, Emma would say he had died in an accident at the lumber mill or he'd been thrown from a horse or any number of easy and plausible explanations. No one would ever question her.

But now, in order to carry out the plan, Emma would have to leave the trunk in the station's baggage area and stay another day to wait for the next train to Jackson. It isn't hard to imagine that the prospect of leaving a trunk with a dead body inside in the depot for another twenty-four hours was too much for almost anybody. Emma lost her nerve. She left the trunk standing on the platform and boarded the next San Francisco train instead, her only thought to get away.

After the train pulled out of the station, the platform was empty except for the trunk. It had no identification and had not been checked. A porter removed it to the baggage room. Several hours later the trunk began emitting an offensive odor that gave the railroad employees the heebie-jeebies. They called the police and an officer opened the trunk, revealing the body of a man, fully dressed and crammed tightly into a folded position, his clothes soaked with blood.

The police summoned the delivery boy who had brought the trunk to the station. He said that he'd transported it from the California Hotel at the request of a female guest. The manager of the hotel was called out to identify the body. It was Albert N. McVicar, he reported, a gentleman who had been staying at the hotel with his wife. The search began for Mrs. McVicar. However, the sheriff soon realized that the suspect went by the name Emma LeDoux, as she was actually the wife of Eugene LeDoux.

The first stop for Stockton Sheriff Walter Sibley on his quest to find Mrs. LeDoux was the Jackson ranch where she lived with her mother Mary Ann Head and stepfather. The search was unfruitful and Mr. and Mrs. Head were less than helpful. However, on March 26 Emma was discovered in Antioch, having checked into a hotel under an alias. She was taken into custody and the grisly details of the murder became public. She knew McVicar was dead, she said, but she didn't kill him. She had been terrorized by being a witness to the murder. Her ex-husband was killed, she said, by a thug named Joe Miller who had come to their hotel room in Stockton, argued with McVicar, poisoned him with carbolic acid, and stolen all his money. Miller had forced Emma to help him dispose of the body, stuffing him into the trunk. Afraid for her life, she had done what he asked, then fled. A bulletin was issued for the arrest of Joseph Miller, though the sheriff was convinced he was fictional, and Emma was taken to the jail in Stockton to await further developments.

After her arrest and during her stay in the Stockton jail, Emma's behavior troubled District Attorney Norton. "I never saw an accused person more cool or unconcerned. She seems to take everything as a matter of course, and is as much interested in what goes on about her as though she were on a pleasure trip or sightseeing. At first glance she is rather good looking, but a study of the face soon develops hardness and cruelty there. She seems to give no thought of the terrible crime with which she is charged."[5] As for Emma's new husband Eugene LeDoux, he was mainly concerned with making sure it all had nothing to do with him. As was the case with the Head family, members of which made public statements to declare that they were of no blood relation to either Mary Head or the accused murderess.

Convinced of Emma's innocence, her mother mortgaged her land and sold enough of her possessions to hire an accomplished lawyer, Charles H. Fairall, for her daughter's defense.

On April 18 the Great Earthquake hit the extended Bay Area, wreaking havoc throughout San Francisco, San Jose, Santa Rosa, and beyond. Many structures that survived the initial shaking of the earth were later destroyed by rampaging fires that resulted from rupturing gas lines. Over 3,000 people were killed and 80% of the city was destroyed. Although the damage in Stockton ninety miles inland was not significant, the disaster greatly impacted the entirety of Northern California. Emma LeDoux's trial, set to start on May 22, was postponed until June.

When the trial did start on June 10, the courtroom drew a crowd of spectators, many of them women, who brought their knitting projects and listened in fascination at the details put forth by the autopsy doctors and the chemist who analyzed the contents of McVicar's stomach. The conclusion was that he died of morphine poisoning. The doctors testified that he was still alive when put in the trunk, as the bleeding that occurred inside the trunk from ruptured vessels in his nose could not have happened after death. The bruises on the man's head also occurred prior to death and most likely were caused when he was dropped into the trunk, probably by being rolled off the bed.

The spectators in the courtroom must have felt cheated when Emma failed to take the stand in her defense. Perhaps her lawyers realized she would be unable to elicit sympathy for two reasons. One, she was a terrible liar, and, two, she didn't seem the least bit distraught about either McVicar's death or her own fate.

There was one day, however, when she lost her composure. Her mother fainted in the courtroom and Emma ran to her side and administered a glass of water. Her mother was then taken out of the room to be cared for and Emma burst into tears.

Her lawyers argued that McVicar had been a drug addict and had either accidentally or on purpose overdosed on morphine and his panicked wife had had a lapse in judgement in trying to get rid of the body. While it was certainly possible that he had taken the morphine himself, the subsequent cool and calculated actions of Emma in her efforts to dispose of the body were supremely incriminating.

The jury didn't buy her defense. After six hours of deliberation, they returned a guilty verdict. Even when the verdict was read, Emma remained calm and then chatted lightheartedly with her attorney.

On August 7 Emma was sentenced to be hanged. At the time, it was often reported that she was the first woman in the history of the Golden State to receive a death sentence. That wasn't true as Laura Fair was sentenced to hang in 1871, though she appealed and avoided that fate.

"The iron nerve of the remarkable little woman," said the Stockton *Record*, "did not fail her at the crucial moment. Except for a tinge of coloring which leaped to her cheeks, and, rapidly rising and falling bosom, she remained the same self-possessed woman that she was throughout the whole nerve-wracking trial." As she was taken from the courtroom and saw her mother, she broke into a fond smile and the two women embraced.

Though Emma was generally stoical in public, she did break down more than once when she was in her jail cell after her sentencing. A San Joaquin County jail cell in those days might have made anybody cry, however, as the cells were dark, tiny, and infested with fleas.

Emma's lawyer appealed based on irregularities with judge and jury, including evidence that one of the jurors had said before the trial began that he believed she was guilty and should "have her neck broke."

In 1907 a rumor began to circulate that Emma was pregnant and about to give birth. The rumor grew and reporters barraged Sheriff Sibley with inquiries until he got fed up and invited the press to interview his prisoner face to face. As soon as they saw her, they knew the rumor was false. She said she had no idea how it got started. "It seems that it is not enough for people to crowd and block the streets to stare at me, as if I were some sort of a Fourth of July horrible; now they must start these rumors."[6]

Despite a reputation as the jail's most cheerful prisoner, Emma lost a lot of weight, grew weak and pale, and began having coughing fits. She was so sickly, in fact, that newspapers reported she was dying of consumption. Doctors were brought in to examine her and concluded that she did not have tuberculosis or any other disease.

On May 19, 1909, the Supreme Court granted Emma a retrial. It had been so long since the original event that the newspapers felt the need to remind people that Emma LeDoux was the "Stockton trunk murderess," which was universally the phrase used. The new trial was scheduled for February 2, 1910, and preparations ensued to round up all the now far flung witnesses.

During the entire four years that had transpired since the death of McVicar, Emma LeDoux had maintained her innocence of the crime. But in January, shortly before her retrial was to begin, she wrote to her attorney, saying, "Owing to the condition of my health, which has become badly shattered by four years' confinement, I do not feel able to stand the strain of another trial. I therefore have decided to plead guilty and I want you to do what you can to dispose of the matter quickly."[7] After entering her new plea, she was sentenced to life in San Quentin. She was thirty-five years old.

When she first arrived at San Quentin, she looked around herself and said to her accompanying matron, "It is a far nicer place than I expected."[8] From all reports, Emma thrived in prison. From their cells, the women could stand on their chairs and see people outside the prison going about their business. Sitting and looking the other way, they could see million dollar views of the San Francisco Bay and the surrounding mountains. Once a month they were taken for a trek over the hills, and in the spring were allowed to go out and pick wildflowers for their rooms. They were allowed to attend baseball games between prison teams, and often had candy pulls. They had a reception room with a piano where they spent leisure time, and were allowed visitors as frequently as people chose to visit. A couple of hours a day they worked at sewing and needlework. Emma was soon put in charge of this work and became a valuable help to the staff. She gained twenty-five pounds during her first year in prison and took up Christian Science. She distinguished herself as a good worker and model prisoner.

Seven years into her incarceration at San Quentin, Emma intervened to stop an attack on Matron Jessie Whalen. A group of angry prisoners made at the matron, the woman in the lead attacking her with a mop handle. Emma quickly interjected herself to wrestle the weapon away and push back the attack, saving the matron's life.

Although prison life agreed with Emma, she applied for a pardon as soon as she was eligible, in 1917. It was denied. The second time she applied it was also denied.

When it began to look like Emma might be paroled in 1920, Eugene LeDoux went to court to have his marriage terminated. Emma was served divorce papers in prison.

She was paroled that same year based on exemplary conduct and because she had saved the life of Matron Whalen. Emma was released into the care of her sister.

But that wasn't the end to Emma's legal missteps. The following year she was arrested and imprisoned again for violating her parole and running a house of prostitution. A couple of years later she was again paroled.

In 1925 she married yet again, to Frederick A. Crackbon, and for the next few years Emma steered clear of trouble. But Crackbon died in 1929 of natural causes (almost certainly).

Emma then opened up a "marriage bureau." For a fee, she interviewed eligible bachelors and set them up with marriageable women, except that she set all of them up with herself. She was then in her fifties. For this con game, she was sent back to prison in 1931.

At that time there were only two state prisons in California, San Quentin and Folsom. In San Quentin, there were fewer than fifty female inmates. In 1932 the California Institute for Women opened south of Bakersfield near

Tehachapi, and the following year 30 female prisoners from San Quentin were relocated there. One of those was Emma LeDoux. She died in prison in 1941 at the age of 66 and was buried in in an unmarked grave in Union Cemetery in Bakersfield.

The blood-stained trunk, however, took on a life of its own that continues to this day. Beginning in 1919, it became part of the annual curiosity display mounted by the sheriff's department at the San Joaquin County Fair. Once the LeDoux case faded out of memory, the trunk remained in storage at the County Jail on the corner of Channel and San Joaquin Streets in Stockton. When the time came to tear down the jailhouse in 1961, the trunk was donated to Stockton's Haggin Museum where it is now prominently displayed under a continuously playing video from the TV show *Mysteries at the Museum*. There the trunk stands open to reveal the ruddy stains on its interior, a grisly memento to one of California's most notorious murders.

I. MURDERERS

The trunk at the Haggin Museum, Stockton, California

II. GAMBLERS AND THIEVES

Prior to the Gold Rush, the major gambling center in the U.S. was New Orleans. An influx of men and women from that city brought the games to San Francisco, which then took over as the nation's gaming center. But every pioneer town in the West had its casinos and gambling halls, and gambling, along with drinking and prostitution, was rampant everywhere the miners went, from the Black Hills of the Dakota Territory to the Comstock Lode of Nevada to the Mother Lode of California. While most gamblers, like most citizens of these places, were men, there were some well-known exceptions. Women were often recruited to work in gambling establishments to serve drinks, spin roulette wheels, and entertain the customers in whatever way was required.

A few of the women who learned the ropes working in casinos, found that they had a talent for gaming. Among the most famous of these was Poker Alice (Alice Ivers Duffield Tubbs Huckert) who was born in England and immigrated with her family to the United States. She became a gambler in South Dakota and opened her own gambling saloon there which included a brothel. Alice was a hard drinker, cigar smoker, bootlegger, and all around bad ass character who claimed that she had won $250,000, an astonishing amount for the time, playing poker. Then there was Kitty Leroy, another legendary gambler, saloon owner, and prostitute who worked in Texas and then in Deadwood, South Dakota. She married five times, ended up killing her third husband and being killed by her fifth. A third notorious female gambler was Eleanor Dumont, known and respected throughout the western United States for her skill at cards. Her story is included in this chapter.

Poker Alice

II. GAMBLERS AND THIEVES

The primary vices that women engaged in during California's early days were prostitution and drinking, and to a lesser extent gambling, but there were a few who indulged in the extremely unladylike crimes of stagecoach hold ups, bank robberies, and pickpocketing. The most famous of these female outlaws is Canadian-born Pearl Hart who became famous for robbing a stagecoach in 1899 in Arizona. After serving time in the Yuma Territorial prison, she worked for a while in Buffalo Bill's Wild West Show. Belle Starr was another notorious outlaw, a bootlegger and horse thief associated with the James-Younger Gang. Her life ended abruptly when she was ambushed on her way home from a dance, shot off her horse with a double-barrel shotgun, then shot again on the ground just to be sure she was dead. The character of Belle Starr evolved into a true Wild West legend. She has appeared in dozens of novels, movies, and television shows.

There were others, like Calamity Jane who, like Belle Starr, got a bright spit-shine to her reputation as time passed. So much so that her story was made into a 1953 musical starring American sweetheart Doris Day. In contrast, the stories that follow are as historically accurate as the surviving sources allow. It's doubtful that any of these women will ever have a movie musical made in their honor; however, their notoriety remains robust.

Pearl Hart, Bandit Queen

ELEANOR DUMONT (1829 – 1879)
"Madame Mustache"

Eleanor Dumont

Eleanor Dumont was known all over the western frontier by the moniker Madame Mustache. Men made special trips, in fact, just to get a look at her, so great was her renown. One of these was steamboat captain Louis Rosche who piloted his ship to Fort Benton, Montana, just so he could sit down at Madame Mustache's *vingt-et-un* (twenty-one) table and lose two hundred dollars. A female gambler was rare enough, but a female dealer was even more rare. Eleanor was both, and she was an expert. When Captain Rosche first saw her in the 1870s, he was surprised to find that she wasn't the beauty legend had promised. He recognized her from the "unbelievable black brush" above her lip. "She was fat," he said, "showing unmistakably the signs of age. Rouge and powder apparently applied only half-heartedly, failed to hide the sagging lines of her face, the pouches under her eyes, the general marks of dissipation. Her one badge of respectability was a black silk dress worn high around her neck."[9] The legend of Eleanor's beauty was true enough, but Rosche was twenty years too late to appreciate it, for Madame was then in her forties.

Over the next hour, Rosche's money moved steadily from his side of the table to neat stacks on Eleanor's side until all of it had been lost. He got up to leave, but Eleanor wasn't finished with him yet. "No, no, no," she said with a marked French accent. "The steamboatman must not go before he has had his drink on the house." She called to the bartender to bring the drink. He placed a glass of milk in front of Rosche. "Your special drink, Mr. Steamboatman," said Madame Mustache with a mischievous gleam in her eyes. Meanwhile, a crowd of onlookers had gathered to laugh at Rosche and his special drink, some of them already in on the gag, since this was Madame's trademark, to set a glass of milk before any sucker she'd cleaned out. There were others on the floor that day who had been similarly served.

There are many colorful stories circulating nowadays about Eleanor Dumont, most of them unverified and doubtless embellished or even dreamt up entirely for their romantic cachet. Storytellers are tempted to invent the details of Eleanor's life because she seems to have sprung fully formed in the Wild West at the age of twenty. Nothing is known of her before she turned up in the Kootenay mining region of British Columbia, already an expert gambler who relieved many a miner of his treasure dealing *vingt-et-un*. She appeared to be French. Many believe that she spent some time in New Orleans where she learned gambling in the glittering gaming palaces of that city.

In 1849 at the age of twenty, she made her way to a budding San Francisco where she first operated a roulette wheel at the Bella Union Hotel. This was the very beginning of the Gold Rush in California. A woman in that town at that time who wasn't a prostitute was a true novelty. In fact, card dealers and players in these places were exclusively men. Eleanor was unique. But the gamblers couldn't have been happier. She was pretty, young, and charming, but she was also untouchable, a woman who was refined, polite, and kept her cool around men. In fact, she had a calming effect on the

II. GAMBLERS AND THIEVES

clientele and prevented more than one brawl by stepping into a scene that was about to get out of hand.

The hordes of men who came to and through San Francisco in those days found little else to entertain themselves with other than women, booze, and gambling, so brothels and gambling houses were as ubiquitous as fast food restaurants are now. But only one of these houses had a woman card dealer. Not for long, however, because the Bella Union began to be overwhelmed with business and the other hotels realized they needed to bring in women as well. Soon nearly every roulette wheel in town was operated by a young woman, and some of the card tables were stocked with them as well, though dealing cards successfully took a level head and experience that many of these trophy women did not possess.

Eleanor's assets for the Bella Union extended beyond her gender. With her French accent and aloof demeanor, she gave a European air to the room, and she always conducted herself like a lady. She was quiet and discreet and kept to herself. Though gambling wasn't illegal, it was considered an unsavory business, unfit for respectable women. In most establishments, in fact, women were not allowed to participate. But Eleanor managed to maintain her dignity despite being a denizen of gambling halls. For her entire life, she commanded respect from anyone who played against her.

In 1854, after a few years working for the man, Eleanor left San Francisco to set herself up in business. She took a stagecoach to the dusty gold rush town of Nevada City, California, where her presence was immediately noticed. A beautiful, fashionably dressed woman traveling alone was an unusual sight in this town. But Eleanor could take care of herself. She owned and carried a gun and knew how to shoot. She was looking for the perfect location for her own business, and she found it on Broad Street. She bought the place and opened "*Vingt-et-un*," named after her favorite card game. Neither women (other than the owner) nor cursing were allowed in the establishment, and customers were expected to be well mannered and politely groomed. Eleanor served free champagne and hired a band to serenade the customers.

Business boomed. It was an upgrade to what the miners were accustomed to and they were happy to lighten their pockets at Eleanor's tables.

With the first place doing so well, Eleanor partnered up with a professional gambler from New York, Dave Tobin, to open another location, Dumont's Palace. Both locations ran around the clock, serving up black jack, faro, and chuck-a-luck. Eleanor and Tobin quarreled about how to run the business until they finally parted ways. Tobin returned to New York with a nice fat chunk of profit from the gambling houses.

When the mines were tapped out in Nevada City, the miners moved on, and Eleanor did the same. She moved to Columbia, California, in 1857 and set up a table in George Foster's City Hotel. The original wood structures of Columbia had recently burned to the ground and been replaced with stone and brick buildings, some of which are still standing today, including the City Hotel, which currently operates as a quaint Victorian-style inn. Columbia truly boomed with ongoing gold strikes throughout the 1850s and 60s, and the men who worked the mines came to town to spend their good fortunes, which in turn left local businesses fat and happy, Eleanor's among them.

While the miners followed the gold strikes, Eleanor followed the miners. Whenever a town dried up, she moved on. She was always the first to know when the gold was petering out by the size of the bets at her table.

In 1859 the discovery of the silver Comstock Lode at Virginia City, Nevada, created a frenzy matched only by the original Gold Rush of California a decade earlier. By the next spring, the "Rush to the Washoe" was on and early investors turned into millionaires overnight. The wealth brought in by the Comstock was said to have been a major source of funding for the Union Army in the Civil War. People poured into Nevada from all points of the globe, drawing in adventurers like Mark Twain, who lived in Virginia City from 1861 to 1864. Having no luck with mining, he supported himself by writing for the local paper, the *Territorial Enterprise*.

Though Eleanor was doing just fine in Columbia, she couldn't ignore the hysteria drummed up by the Rush to the

II. GAMBLERS AND THIEVES

Washoe. It was like a tsunami sweeping everybody further inland. She always wanted to be where the action was, so she set up her table in Virginia City and raked in the profits. The next move she made was in September 1861. Pioche, Nevada put itself on the map as the latest mining district to boom. Unlike Virginia City, Pioche was a hell-raising, lawless place in an isolated area of the country. It was in Pioche that Eleanor met Jack McKnight, a dashing cattle buyer who swept her off her feet. Eleanor had often expressed a desire to give up gambling and settle down to a quiet life, and now that she was in her thirties, the time seemed right. She had the money and she had a man. In 1863 she bought a cattle ranch near Carson City, Nevada, for the two of them to work together. But McKnight turned out to be a swindler. He squandered all of Eleanor's money and sold the ranch out from under her, running off with the profit and leaving her with nothing.

After McKnight left the scene, an embittered Eleanor returned to gambling. She also started drinking heavily. She gained weight and the peach fuzz on her upper lip coarsened and darkened, gaining her the distinctive nickname by which she would become famously known, Madame Mustache.

Despite the setback, she had soon made enough money to buy a gambling house in Bannack, Montana. It included a brothel upstairs, so she became a madam as well as a gambler. One of the young women who worked for Eleanor in Bannack was fifteen year old Martha Jane Cannary, better known as Calamity Jane. Eleanor taught Jane the ropes of gambling, though Jane always had a reputation as a lousy gambler. "Their house was a popular resort," said Charles W. Bocker, a regular, "and Calamity Jane was everybody's girl."[10]

Jane and Eleanor developed a lasting friendship, with Jane tagging along for a while as Eleanor followed the miners. During the 1870s, she moved often, going to Helena, Butte, Bozeman, and Fort Benton in Montana, then Salmon, Idaho, and Deadwood, South Dakota.

Deadwood came alive in 1876 when gold was discovered in the Black Hills. The usual masses streamed in, and, along with them, Madame Mustache arrived to play twenty-one.

Calamity Jane, c. 1880 (Photo by C. E. Finn)

Eleanor was at the height of her fame in Deadwood. She was described in the local paper as follows: "A character who attracts the attention of all strangers is 'Mme. Moustache,' a plump little French lady, perhaps forty years of age, but splendidly preserved. She derives her name, which is the only one she is known by, from a dainty strip of black hair upon her upper lip. She deals her own faro bank, and is quite popular with the boys, who treat her with marked respect. She has bright black eyes and a musical voice, and there is something attractive about her as she looks up with a little smile and says, 'You will play, M'sieur?'" The article continued by saying, "No one knows her history, which would probably be very romantic if correctly written."

Calamity Jane was also in Deadwood at this time. An old timer who knew both women, George Hoshier, owner of a natural lithium spring near town, recalled that Calamity Jane had two very special friends, Madame Mustache and Stem Winder, another female card dealer. Of Eleanor, Hoshier said "She was probably the best known woman then in all the West...She was better known that Calamity was."[11]

Deadwood was at the center of the action in 1877, so it isn't surprising that another celebrated character also rode into town that year. It turned out to be a fateful move for western folk hero Wild Bill Hickok. As he played poker on August 2, 1877, at Carl Mann's saloon, he was shot and killed by Jack McCall. McCall was later hanged for the crime.

As Eleanor aged, her air of refinement went the way of her smooth upper lip. She grew coarser, using foul language and smoking cigars. For drink, she'd turned from champagne to whiskey. As she traveled from town to town, her name preceded her, and the gamblers turned out to have a go at her tables and get a look at the legendary woman. Though she was at the height of her fame, she was no longer at the height of her game. She was losing more frequently than in the past, as liquor was ruining her talents.

In May 1878 she returned to California, settling in the tiny ramshackle mining town of Bodie, and worked a twenty-one table in the Magnolia Saloon. At that time, Bodie had a reputation as the most lawless town in Eastern California, a gritty place with over thirty saloons and regular homicides. Eleanor's arrival was heralded in the Bodie *Standard* with the words: "Madame Mustache, whose real name is Eleanore Dumont, has settled for the time in Bodie, following her old avocation of dealing twenty-one, faro, etc., as force of circumstances seem to demand. Probably no woman on the Coast is better known. She has been in a great many of the camps when at their height of prosperity and excitement, and remained until there was hardly a dog left to wail out the dismal story of their desertion. She appears as young as ever, and those who knew her ever so many years ago would instantly recognize her now."

Eleanor made an unremarkable living in Bodie for about a year. But one night things went sour for the fifty year old dealer and she had to borrow $300 from a friend to keep her table open. But her luck had run out and she lost the bank. She left the saloon and wandered out of town, where she drank a cocktail of claret and morphine and collapsed. She was found dead by a sheepherder on September 8, 1879, along with a note saying she was "tired of life."

The *Bodie Morning News* reported her death on September 9:

> Yesterday morning a sheep-herder, while in pursuit of his avocation, discovered the dead body of a woman lying about one hundred yards from the Bridgeport road, a mile from town. Her head rested on a stone, and the appearance of the body indicated that death was the result of natural causes. Ex-officio Coroner Justice Peterson was at once notified, and he dispatched a wagon in charge of H.Ward [of the Pioneer Furniture Store] to that place, who brought the body to the undertaking rooms. Deceased was named Eleanore Dumont, and was recognized as the woman who had been engaged in dealing a twenty-one game in the Magnolia saloon. Her death evidently occurred from an overdose of morphine, an empty bottle having the peculiar smell of that drug, being found beside the body... The history connected with the unfortunate suicide is but a repetition of that of many others who have followed the life of a female gambler, with the exception perhaps that the subject of this item bore a character for virtue possessed by few in her line. To the goodhearted women of the town must we accord praise for their accustomed kindness in doing all in their power to prepare the unfortunate woman's body for burial.

II. GAMBLERS AND THIEVES

The locals raised enough money to provide Eleanor with a proper burial, which was later described by George A. Montrose, an attorney and former editor of the Bridgeport *Chronicle-Union*: "She had the reputation of being honest in her dealings and always paying her debts. Upon this she prided herself, and woe unto anyone who claimed she did not play fair... It is said that of the hundreds of funerals held in the mining camp, that of 'Madame Mustache' was the largest. The gamblers of the place buried her with all honors, and carriages were brought from Carson City, Nevada, a distance of 120 miles, especially to be used in the funeral cortege."

Like many of the towns that Eleanor worked in, Bodie, California, is now a ghost town, isolated and rusting into the landscape. It is mournfully quiet, disturbed only by scurrying fence lizards and an occasional passing tumbleweed. It's a state park now, and one of the more interesting Western ghost towns to visit. While you're there, keep in mind that one of the ghosts roaming the dusty streets is a plump French woman with a thin mustache and a handful of face cards. Peer into the window of a decrepit saloon and listen. You might just hear a mischievous voice inquire, "You will play, M'sieur?"

MABEL KEATING (1870 - ?)
"The Queen of the Pickpockets"

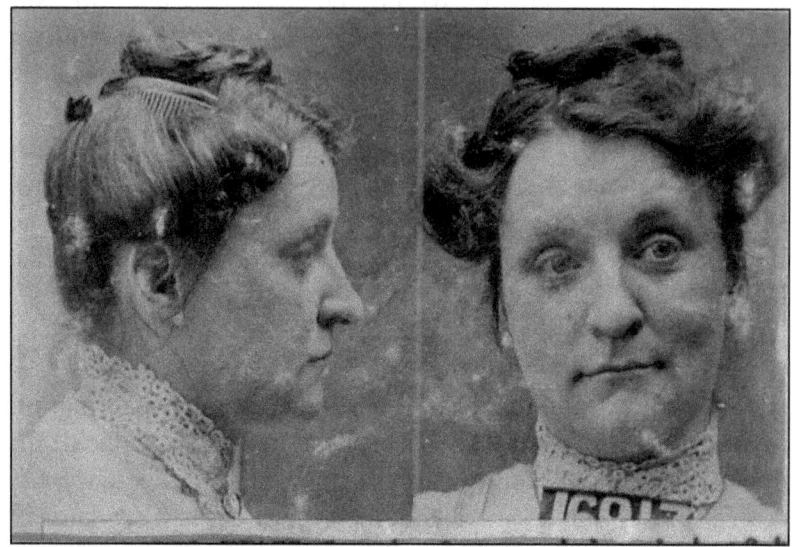

Mabel Keating (Bancroft Library)

Mabel Keating changed her name often. She was sometimes known as Mabel Armstrong, sometimes Mabel Gorman, Mabel Tierney, Mabel Wood, or Mabel White. Who she was originally, before she turned to a life of crime, is not a matter of record. In the spring of 1891 when she showed up in Sacramento, California, she was about twenty-one years old, had hazel eyes and light brown hair, called herself Mabel Armstrong, and was in the company of her lover or husband, James Keating. By this time, she was already a master at deftly picking a pocket without alerting the pocket's owner. For the brief time she worked in downtown Sacramento, her turf was Second Street between K and L.

She was so incredibly successful at her chosen profession that her income during her most active years, the 1890s, was estimated to be a whopping $25,000 a year.

After Sacramento, Mabel moved to San Francisco to ply her trade. Her first arrest was in 1892 for stealing $90 from a touring mind reader. He had to leave town and was unable to press his case, so Mabel was charged only with vagrancy.

She took only cash, coins and bills, and by the age of twenty-six had stolen as much as $300,000 from San Francisco's men about town. In those days, people's comings and goings, at least among the high society types, were published in the newspapers. This allowed Mabel to monitor the arrival of wealthy men and watch their habits, preying on many while they were entertaining themselves in the Tenderloin District with liquor and women. After a binge like that, many of Mabel's targets wouldn't have any idea what had happened to their money, nor would they want to draw attention to where they'd been and what they'd been doing when they lost it.

Her usual method of obtaining coins was to cut open a pocket with a small pen knife and take the money or take it without cutting the pocket and replace it with brass counters. She usually went about this business in the evenings on Geary, Post, and Sutter streets. After each hit, Mabel went home to change her hairdo and her clothes and put on different jewelry, so as to alter the description anyone might give the police and to make her less recognizable. She loved her sealskin jacket, however, and wore it nearly every time she went out. It was the one item that was standard about her appearance. The San Francisco *Examiner* described her technique as follows: "She chooses her victims with the care that a hunter exercises when, having a herd of game before him, he selects only the sleek animals as his targets."[12] This method of selective targeting proved highly lucrative.

From December 1893 until May 1897 Mabel was arrested and charged with grand larceny twelve times. Every one of the cases was dismissed. She had a way of convincing a jury that she was being victimized by her male accusers. The jurors, being male themselves, were sympathetic to the young, pretty, weeping Mabel and let her off. The vast majority of her victims never reported the crime. They didn't want to get involved in a court case or admit that they had been robbed. It was preferable to just accept the loss. Another way she escaped jail time when caught was to offer to give the money back if her mark agreed not to prosecute. In many cases, they agreed. She also had a gang of friends who were ready to come to court and swear that she was with them at the time of the alleged crime. These same friends took it upon themselves when required to threaten witnesses and scare them away from the witness stand. Many times nobody showed up when the time came to testify.

In 1893 Mabel went into partnership with her friend Annie Piggott, another notorious San Francisco pickpocket, to work the Chicago World's Fair. They robbed mostly visitors to Chicago, victims who were unable to stay in town to prosecute. From one Louisville bookie, Mabel lifted $1,000. He declined to report the crime. It was a profitable trip. After the fair, she and Annie came home to San Francisco and continued doing what they did best.

In 1895 Frank Gorman, a felon and all-around bad apple, broke into Mabel's apartment, knocked her down, and stole several valuable items of clothing, including her favorite sealskin jacket, which he pawned at a shop on Grant Street for $50. He also took an overcoat that he claimed was his, suggesting that this wasn't his first encounter with Mabel. Nor would it be his last. Mabel wasn't above cheating on James Keating, and despite Gorman's ungentlemanly behavior, he had a certain charm for Mabel.

By the age of twenty-six, Mabel had become famous for her light-fingered capers and was featured in an article in the *Examiner*, in which she was dubbed "Queen of the Pickpockets." The title stuck. "The exploits of this woman have come to be the wonder of the detectives. She is but twenty-six years old, of good looks, a charming manner and an ability to detect with a single glance of her hazel eyes the weak points in a man's nature. These gifts, coupled with a marvelous deftness of touch, make her the most adept and dangerous of all the women of her class."[13]

In 1898 Mabel began an affair with City Hall janitor Jerry Sullivan. When James Keating found out about it, he accosted Sullivan and told him to stay away from his wife. Mabel sent Sullivan a note telling him it was over, that her husband might kill him if he didn't stay away. But Sullivan defiantly strolled

II. GAMBLERS AND THIEVES 51

into the Keating bar on March 6 and demanded a drink. James Keating said he wouldn't serve him until he paid off his bill, which Sullivan refused to do. An argument ensued. Mabel stepped between them and attempted to calm the situation, but her interference had the opposite effect. Sullivan pulled out his pistol and shot both Keatings, Mabel in the chest and James through the back of the neck. They both recovered, but Mabel was seriously injured and the bullet was never removed from her body. In custody, Jerry Sullivan said he was sorry he hadn't killed them both. In the manner of the time and place, he was convicted of simple assault and sentenced to three months in the County Jail.

Later that year, on May 3, James Keating died of tuberculosis.

By now, Mabel was so well known to the public and the police that continuing her business in San Francisco was tricky. She moved to Sacramento briefly, but that city ordered her out. She next turned up in Seattle where, as Mabel Wilson, she continued her old tricks. Interestingly, her old friend in crime Annie Piggott also relocated to Seattle during this time.

But Mabel wasn't as lucky there as she had always been in San Francisco. In April 1901 she was arrested for stealing $5. She was convicted and sentenced to 30 days in jail. In September she was arrested for stealing $20. She offered to pay the money back, which had often worked for her in the past, but in this case was seen merely as evidence of her guilt. An attempt by her lawyer to bribe a juror also backfired. Mabel was convicted of grand larceny. She was sentenced to two years in state prison, her first prison term. She served her time and when she was released, she returned to San Francisco, perhaps thinking her old haunts would be more welcoming than Seattle had been.

She went by the name of May Gorman, as she was now in a relationship with Frank Gorman. She was picked up by police in May 1904 for a three-dollar robbery. The authorities weren't fooled by her name change. They recognized Mabel Keating right away. Though she was acquitted for the robbery, she was taken to jail to be held until she promised to leave the city. She didn't keep that promise, however, and the next time she was arrested, in June 1905, she was again told to leave and said she would, that she was off to Portland to work the Exposition there. But there was just something about San Francisco for Mabel. It was home, after all, and she stayed put.

Not long after that last arrest, Mabel and Frank tried to start a legitimate business, a chicken ranch in the Richmond District, and she dropped out of the news, apparently having retired from crime at the age of 35.

Frank, however, was still taking things that didn't belong to him, often in the company of his buddies Joseph Riordan and C. E. Horton. The three of them were responsible for a series of burglaries and holdups. They had great success until April 1909 when their luck ran out. Frank entered the office of the Thompson bridge company, shot the president non-fatally and relieved him of a bag containing $3,200 in payroll money. He fled in Mabel's horse and buggy through the streets of San Francisco, shooting at several policemen who were in hot pursuit. Eventually, he was apprehended.

Mabel and her sister visited Frank every day in jail while he awaited his trial. Frank was convicted and sentenced to fifty years in San Quentin. When the sentence was announced, Mabel bolted up from her seat and fled the courtroom in tears.

It's likely that Mabel took another name after Gorman's conviction, but, retired from thievery, she kept a low profile for the rest of her life, and nothing is known of her in retirement. Where she originally came from and where she ended up remain a mystery, but her reputation on the West Coast as Queen of the Pickpockets is as alive as it ever was.

JUANITA SPINELLI (1889 – 1941)
"The Duchess"

Juanita Spinelli, 1941

We can't say goodbye to notorious thieves without spending some time with the most notorious of them all. Evelita Juanita Spinelli was about as hard as they come, described by FBI profiler Candice DeLong as "a stone cold psychopath who had no use for anybody, other than what she could get out of them." She had at various times worked as a waitress, a wrestler, a madam, roulette wheel spinner, odd jobs at a carnival, or whatever would pay the bills, but her true calling was as a petty gangster. She had the skills, the nerve, and the brutal callousness for a life of crime. One of her specialties was making homemade blackjacks to whack people over the head with. Another was knife throwing. She was reportedly able to pin a poker chip with a knife at fifteen paces.

Juanita's life up until the age of fifty consists of a murky collection of snapshots. The best account comes from her son Joseph, who told what he could remember of his mother's rambling life in 1941 when he was 19. Between his memories and a few facts revealed by Juanita herself, we can sketch the following with some confidence.

Juanita was born in Kentucky, October 17, 1889. She married several times. Her children weren't even sure how many. By her husband Spinelli, she had two children, daughter Lorraine, nicknamed Gypsy, and son Joseph who never met his father. When Joseph was very young, Juanita worked as a waitress and washerwoman in the oil fields of Texas. The children went to school in short stints, but not regularly, as the family was always on the move, their mode of travel nearly always hitchhiking. They went to Salt Lake City and joined a carnival where Juanita ran a gambling wheel and Lorraine was a "snake girl" in a sideshow. When they quit the show, they hitchhiked north to Kilgore, Idaho, and settled for a time on a sheep ranch owned by a man named Robinson. Joseph vaguely recalled that his mother may have married him. Around 1930 Juanita left her kids in a Catholic children's home in Texas and went to Mexico where she married a bank robber. After he was killed, she returned with another son, Vincent, born in 1931. She then picked up the other kids and hitched to Detroit.

That's where she got involved with the notorious "Purple Gang" terrorist group, one of the most active and violent gangs in Detroit. By the end of the 1920s, the Purple Gang was on top. They controlled the vice, gambling, liquor, and drug trades. They demanded protection money from the entire

II. GAMBLERS AND THIEVES

dry cleaning industry in Detroit and used arson and murder to keep the businesses in line. By the time Juanita joined the gang, they had begun to weaken due to sloppiness, cockiness, and infighting. Juanita wasn't a boss of this gang, but she was underworld nobility, high enough to earn the nickname "The Duchess." Gang members were bootleggers and truck hijackers, committing armed robberies and often lifting bootleg liquor from other gangs. They also kidnapped members of other gangs and held them for ransom. It was a tough scene where a tough woman got even tougher.

It was in Detroit that Juanita met Mike Simeone, twenty years her junior, when he volunteered to be a fourth in a pinochle game she was playing. They fell in love.

The Purple Gang became an even more dangerous scene as it fell apart. Various members fingered various other members to escape prosecution. There is evidence that Juanita sold out some of the bigger boys involved in the laundry racket murders and fled Detroit to escape the vengeance of the gang. If that wasn't sufficient reason to get out, another reason presented itself when daughter Lorraine ran away from home in 1937. She made her way to San Francisco, then contacted her mother to let her know she was doing fine. Juanita, now nearing 50, packed up what was left of her family and followed, anxious for new horizons. Simeone joined them.

Lorraine had meanwhile become acquainted with juvenile delinquents Albert Ives, Gordon Hawkins, and nineteen year old Robert Sherrod. These boys became the Spinelli gang. Juanita taught them how to make and use blackjacks, how to use knives and guns, how to overpower and lay out a victim. They then set to work stealing cars and robbing small businesses. Though the men did most of the dirty work, there was no question that Juanita was calling the shots.

In April 1940 Robert Sherrod and one-eyed Albert Ives held up Leland Cash, a barbecue stand owner on the Embarcadero. They had planned a routine stick up like all the others. But Cash was partially deaf, so he didn't understand what he was being ordered to do. He acted too slowly for the jumpy Sherrod, who shot and killed him.

Afterward, Sherrod couldn't stop dwelling on the incident or talking about it. The gang stole a car and drove to Sacramento, Sherrod all the while babbling about what was going to happen to him if they got caught. Juanita and Simeone were afraid of his loose tongue, so they decided he was too great a liability. They took him to a hotel room and gave him whiskey dosed with chloral hydrate to knock him out. Once he was unconscious, the men took off his clothes and dressed him in a pair of swimming trunks. They put him in the trunk of the car and drove to the Freeport Bridge over the Sacramento River. Ives threw him over the side of the bridge. He drowned.

From Sacramento, the gang drove to Reno. Ives thought he overheard the others talking about ways to get rid of him too, so he made a break for it and confessed everything to the police. The gang was arrested in Truckee, California.

Under questioning, Juanita expressed her disappointment in Ives, saying she had planned to stick a long hatpin in his ear, but he squealed before she had a chance.

The Sacramento police went whole hog into the investigation, pursuing every lead, past and present, and following the trail of Juanita Spinelli back in time to unearth a long career of underworld activity. What they discovered was a shockingly vicious history of crime, and they realized that this was their chance to get this hardened villain behind bars for good. But not just Juanita. Mike Simeone was just as bad. He had served five years in Leavenworth on white slavery charges, and, according to Juanita, once he got out, he went right back at it, pimping out and blackmailing women.

Juanita, Ives, and Hawkins all pled innocent by reason of insanity. Simeone just pled innocent. Juanita and Hawkins were ruled sane. Ives, who had spent some time previously in a mental institution, was ruled insane.

During the trial, Juanita tried to paint herself as a victim of the hard-boiled men she'd gotten mixed up with, namely Ives. She said he was a cold-blooded killer and he'd threatened to send her daughter Lorraine to work in a Chinese prostitution house if she didn't cooperate with his criminal pursuits. The attempted robbery of Cash, she said, was also his idea, and he acted entirely without her knowledge. About the killing of Sherrod, she said Ives had engineered the entire thing because the boy talked too much. She denied that she was the ringleader. "I was forced to stay with them," she said. As to the murder of Sherrod, all she admitted to was putting the knockout drops in his drink. "I put the knockout drops in his glass. I knew they were going to kill him and I didn't want him to feel it. Bob was a good kid."[14]

Ives contradicted that testimony, saying he got his orders from Simeone and Spinelli, and that on the drive to Reno, he had been spooked when he overheard them talking about how to get rid of him, maybe by throwing him off a cliff in the high Sierras.

For his part, Gordon Hawkins described how he'd met Juanita in San Francisco about a year earlier and he was at first treated like one of the family. Then, after he overheard them talking about the Purple Gang and jobs they'd done, they told him he'd be hung if he talked. "I never left the gang alone after that," he said. "There'd always be another guy with me." He admitted to driving the car they took to the bridge where Sherrod was dumped.

Simeone admitted to pouring the whisky, but said he didn't know about the knockout drops. He was just trying to calm Sherrod down, he said, with a harmless drink.

Conveniently, the only person to admit to having a hand in Sherrod's death was Ives, the one member of the gang who had been deemed insane. He confessed to throwing the unconscious Ives off the bridge.

Juanita, 51, Mike Simeone, 33, and Gordon Hawkins, 22, were all found guilty of first degree murder. The only problem the five women and seven men of the jury had with the decision was the uneasiness of some jurors about giving a woman a death sentence. No woman had ever been put to death in California by the courts except one who had basically been railroaded through a pathetic miners' court and lynched (Josefa Segovia—Chapter I). In the end the jurors all agreed and withheld a recommendation of life imprisonment, making the death sentence mandatory.

Albert Ives was sent to the Mendocino state hospital. Juanita was scheduled to die in the San Quentin gas chamber on June 20, 1940, at 10 a.m. She was taken to the women's prison in Tehachapi to await her execution. While she was there, her daughter boasted that she "would get a gang together and spring mother from prison." Security around Juanita was increased as a result.

Interestingly, eleven male prisoners at San Quentin sent a petition to Governor Culbert Olson asking him to spare Juanita's life and offering to draw straws for one of them to take her place in the gas chamber. Their reason was that they felt no woman, especially a mother, should be executed. Juanita's son Vincent was only nine years old at the time. He and his sixteen year old brother were sent to an orphanage after their mother's arrest. Lorraine was 18, an adult. She was also pregnant, due to give birth in August.

At the last minute, on June 19, after Juanita had been brought to San Quentin to face the gas chamber, Governor Olson granted her a thirty-day reprieve based on a claim that new information about the case had come to light. Juanita was awakened and given the news. She fell to her knees and said, "Thank God. He has listened to my prayer. I hope he will find a way to get the truth. Perhaps Mike will tell the truth now. I have prayed hard today and tonight."[15]

Juanita then spoke lightheartedly to reporters on a variety of topics, sitting outside the gas chamber, a tiny, graying, plain-looking woman wearing glasses and a simple jumper. She said she hated the nickname "The Duchess." She said she was no duchess, no murderess, but just misunderstood. She was a persecuted, widowed mother of three children. She went on to say that Mike Simeone was responsible for ruining her life. He had forced her to do his bidding by threatening to hurt or kill her children.

But the hearing that followed with Judge Raymond Coughlin revealed no new evidence or any valid justification for reopening the case. The Judge was irritated and felt that he and the governor had been misused. The governor had an hour long chat with Juanita's son Joseph, hoping to get a clearer picture of his mother. What he heard was a sordid story of a

II. GAMBLERS AND THIEVES

disjointed, nomadic childhood. The governor had a talk with Juanita as well.

On July 17 Olson again granted a 30-day reprieve for The Duchess and the others, saying he hadn't had time to give the case the attention it deserved. When the time came around again in August for the executions, Governor Olson issued a third stay, this time for 90 days. That put the new execution date at November 21. By this time, the disgruntled public opinion was that Juanita Spinelli would never see her execution day.

Juanita also continued to believe that the death penalty would not be carried out. After all, executing a woman was unheard of. And after three stays, surely the governor did not intend to let her go to the gas chamber. On November 19 Governor Olson issued a statement saying that he had given the case a great deal of thought, but had found no reason to commute the sentence to life imprisonment. "The conclusion seems inescapable," he said, "that she willfully and premeditatedly joined with others in the commission of the murder and was a principal in the crimes and criminal purposes of her boy and associates."[16]

A car was sent from San Quentin to Tehachapi to pick up Juanita and bring her back to San Francisco on Thanksgiving Day. The warden allowed her a press conference. She appeared before the reporters, haggard, pale, her dark hair streaked with gray. She blamed police propaganda for her plight and bitterly denounced the people who would not help her. "Some of my blood will burn holes in their bodies," she said.

Juanita spent her last night in hysterics, screaming, banging on the walls and tearing a handful of hair from her head. Even as this was taking place, her lawyers were still trying to save her. They had made an appeal to the Supreme Court on the basis that the gas chamber was "cruel and unusual punishment." Minutes before the time of the execution, the court denied the motion without comment. The time was up and Juanita's options had run out.

The morning of November 21, The Duchess was half carried into the gas chamber by two guards as she muttered futile prayers and carried photos of her children and her infant grandchild next to her bosom. She died at 10:25 a.m. within seconds of the gas being turned on. She was 52 years old. Juanita was buried in Mt. Olivet Catholic Cemetery in San Rafael.

Mike Simeone and Gordon Hawkins were executed on November 28. They came into the gas chamber cocky and joking. They shook hands with their guards before being strapped into the chairs, then gamely tried to keep the smiles on their lips as they followed their leader into oblivion.

Juanita Spinelli's unenviable claim to fame will never be usurped. She was and always will be the first female legally executed in California.

II. GAMBLERS AND THIEVES

Juanita Spinelli

III. HEIRESSES

Freedom of choice for women in the 1800s was severely limited. Success for women was primarily determined by how well they married. If they didn't marry, they often became a burden to one of their siblings, the proverbial "maiden aunt." But there was a class of woman for whom such societal pressures and expectations were inconsequential. These were the fortunate few to be born into money, the heiresses. Their inheritance guaranteed that they would never have to fret about paying the bills. But wealth gave them more than financial security. It gave them the heady freedom to live as they wished. Far from worrying about marrying well, these women needn't marry at all if that was their choice. As women have always known, the value of not having to rely on or be accountable to another person is a massive advantage in life. This was especially true for those who had eccentric inclinations, as did the two women in this chapter. They could indulge such inclinations because they had nothing to fear from those who disapproved. Nobody had any power over them. Their immense wealth gave them the freedom to ignore the expectations of society and forge their own sometimes bizarre life journeys.

As we see throughout this book, there were many ways a woman could write her own rules in the 1800s, though not all of them can be recommended. For the women in this chapter, however, their legacies are generally positive. Lillie Hitchcock Coit, for example, could reasonably be called the patron saint of San Francisco. These women raised many an eyebrow, upset the status quo, and certainly became notorious, but all in all they did no serious harm and broke only a few minor laws, leaving us with some rollicking good stories.

LILLIE HITCHCOCK COIT (1843 - 1929)
"Firebell Lillie"

Lillie Hitchcock Coit (Bancroft Library)

Standing atop Telegraph Hill, elegant Coit Tower is one of the most recognizable landmarks in San Francisco, but its backstory is less well known. It is a love story between a city and a woman, a remarkable woman with a free and ferocious spirit who blazed a singular trail through life and left an eternal legacy to her beloved San Francisco.

Lillie was born Elizabeth Wyche Hitchcock in 1843 in West Point, New York, the only child of an Army doctor from South Carolina, Charles M. Hitchcock, and Martha Hunter. But Lillie's story really began with a terrifying fire at her home in San Francisco on December 23, 1851. An eight-year-old child living with her parents in the Oriental Hotel at Battery and Bush, she was rescued from the fire by volunteer firefighter John Boynton of the Knickerbocker Engine Company #5, a company organized by New Yorkers in 1850.

Fires were commonplace in the early city, as so many of the buildings were constructed of wood, and Lillie had always been drawn to the excitement surrounding the rush to the fire. In those days, volunteer firefighters pulled the engine with ropes, which must have been a challenge on the hills of San Francisco. Whenever Lillie heard a fire bell, she came running. After surviving her own fire, "Firebell Lillie" became the mascot of Knickerbocker Engine Company #5 on Sacramento Street. She could often be seen perched atop the engine as it sped through the city. She spent her free time at the firehouse, hanging out with her heroes. As she got older, she even sometimes took her turn at pulling the fire engine and pumping water.

When the Civil War broke out, Lillie embarrassed her family by being unabashedly for the South, so her father shipped her off to Paris. Now nineteen, Lillie became friends with Empress Eugenie, who employed her as a translator of documents from the United States and entertained her with balls at the Tuileries palace. After two years abroad, she returned to San Francisco and promptly returned to her firehouse hangout.

Glad of her return, the engine company voted her in as the first female firefighter in California in 1863. They gave her a badge and a hat and coat and welcomed the dashing brunette into their ranks. Dressing as a man, playing poker and smoking cigars, Lillie, then a young woman in her early twenties, managed to fit right in. She was so proud of her firefighter status that for many years after she quit fighting fires, she embroidered #5 on all of her underwear.

In addition to riding on firetrucks and wearing men's trousers, Lillie's behavior in general was considered extremely eccentric. She was a sharp billiard player and could take most men, and when she went to Silver Sulphur Springs in St. Helena on vacation, she had a habit of riding on top of the train engine as it traveled through the Napa Valley, shocking

III. HEIRESSES

the staid women along the way who didn't know what to make of her because "girls didn't do such things."

A vivid and well-remembered example of Lillie's devotion to her firemen occurred one evening when a fire broke out at Post and Market Streets while she was attending the opera. Hearing the sirens, she immediately flew from the opera house in her evening dress and cloak and chased the fire engine to the scene. She begged to hold the hose pipe and the firemen obliged her. When the air chamber of the engine suddenly burst, the firewoman, in her linen and lace, was drenched. As usual, she took it with good humor.

Though she shocked many people, in general Lillie was well loved by San Franciscans. She was admired at a time when going against the prevailing wind was not much tolerated. When she was criticized, it wasn't in public, and she maintained her position in high society. It was said that she could entertain twenty gentlemen at once with her vivacious powers of conversation.

At the age of twenty-five she abruptly married Howard Coit, son of Dr. B. B. Coit, a friend of her father's, surprising Pacific Coast society as well as her parents. They immediately packed her off to Europe, their solution to local embarrassments, while the bridegroom remained in San Francisco. "This last act," reported the *Sacramento Daily Union*, "was in keeping with her usual romantic, unlike-anybody-else style of doing." One of Lillie's intimate female friends told reporters that Lillie married Coit to give herself freedom from her parents. As a married woman, she could do as and go where she pleased with a chaperone and without her parents breathing down her neck. The *Stockton Daily Independent* responded to this explanation with, "This is hardly probable…because she would do as she pleased anyhow."

By 1879, the couple had separated, but they never divorced. When Dr. Hitchcock died in 1885 he left his daughter an allowance of only $250 a month as long as her husband lived, after which she would receive the rest of her inheritance. Oddly enough, Howard Coit died a few days after Dr. Hitchcock, and Lillie inherited half of the Hitchcock estate, valued at a quarter million dollars, an immense fortune at the time.

Throughout her life, Lillie maintained a warm and special relationship with firemen. She was always quick to offer help if a fireman needed it. She furnished coffee and food at the end of a hard-fought fire and would visit and send gifts to ill and injured firefighters and their family members. She had a diamond pin in the shape of a five that she always wore to commemorate her favorite engine company. She maintained a soft spot for them throughout her life and they felt the same toward her.

Lillie continued to live the good life, traveling around the world, frequently with her mother, keeping sumptuous apartments in San Francisco and Paris, and ranches in Calistoga and the Napa Valley. She spent her time in the company of the world's rich and famous, but she was big-hearted and generous, and her spirited escapades were received with good humor. She remained forever loyal to her "fireboys," always making an appearance at the annual fireman's banquet if she was in town. If she was out of state, she sent a big floral arrangement instead.

Like so many old San Francisco stories, this one includes a scandal at the magnificent Palace Hotel, the home of only the most well-heeled San Francisco residents and visitors. Lillie had rooms there in the 1890s and early 1900s. One day she was in her parlor in the company of Major J. W. McClure when her cousin Alexander Garnett arrived, inebriated, and the two men started arguing. Garnett pulled a gun and shot McClure, who died the next day. Lillie hightailed it to Europe until things quieted down.

Lillie's mother, with whom she remained close, kept detailed diaries of all of the family exploits, including Lillie's adventures, scandalous or not. Over the years, she was given many handsome offers to publish the diaries, but refused, explaining that they would have to be edited so radically for publication that nothing of interest would remain.

As Lillie aged, she settled down considerably and no longer made headlines, but San Franciscans remained eager for news of her throughout her life. Her youthful escapades had established her as an enduring local legend.

She spent much of her later life in Paris where her daily routine in her 70s included a long walk into the country, between five and ten miles. Her chauffeur followed her in the car in case she should need it, but generally she did not. When WWI broke out, she remained in France and devoted herself to tending to wounded soldiers. Toward the end of her life she returned to San Francisco.

Coit Tower (Library of Congress)

When Lillie died on July 22, 1929, aged 85, the funeral was held at Grace Cathedral. Firemen marched in the procession to Cypress Lawn Cemetery where her headstone contains the words, "Lillie Hitchcock Coit, 5."

Lillie left a third of her massive fortune to the city of San Francisco. The money was used to build Coit Tower, completed in 1933, a distinctive beacon on the skyline of San Francisco to be recognized and admired by generations of visitors and residents alike. The tower was designed by the architectural firm of Arthur Brown, Jr. It's a fitting memorial to the high-spirited philanthropist whose love of San Francisco and its firefighters stayed foremost in her heart throughout her life and beyond. The remaining funds were used to erect a memorial to the Volunteer Fire Department (1849 – 1866) in Washington Square.

AIMEE CROCKER (1863 – 1941)
"The Queen of Bohemia"

Aimee Crocker (Library of Congress)

Amy Isabella Crocker was an heiress and bon vivant, a convention defying woman during a most conventional age. She was a fearless adventurer, thrill seeker, and socialite, and a collector of fine jewels, lovers and husbands. In many biographical sketches during her lifetime, she was predictably summed up by listing the variety and number of her spouses. But her life was so much more interesting than her collection of surnames. She said as much herself when interviewed on the publication of her autobiography, *I'd Do It All Again* (Coward McCann, 1936), which, to the dismay of many of her contemporaries, barely mentioned her five marriages. But there was plenty of material to fill the book, as Amy had become one of the most outrageous, colorful and famous characters of her time, known throughout the world for her outré behavior and bold escapades. Amy declared that the true art of humanity was living. If so, she was the consummate artist.

Born into a wealthy and powerful family on April 18, 1863, Amy Isabella Crocker had every advantage in life. She had a fortune at her disposal, and if she wanted to do nothing else with her life than entertain herself, she was free to do so. Which is essentially what she did.

The Crocker family was well known in both San Francisco and in Sacramento where Amy was born. Her uncle, Charles Crocker, was one of the "Big Four" railroad tycoons of California, the other three being Leland Stanford, Mark Hopkins, and Collis Potter Huntington. Amy's father Edwin became the principal attorney for the Central Pacific Railroad and did okay for himself. In 1868 he bought property at Third and O Streets in Sacramento and hired architect Seth Babson to design an Italianate mansion and a gallery building to house the family's large art collection. The gallery building included a bowling alley, skating rink and billiards room on the ground floor, a natural history museum and a library on the first floor, and gallery space on the second floor. Completed in 1872, the Crocker family mansion and art gallery are considered the masterpieces of Babson's career.

Amy was raised in both Sacramento and San Francisco amid the highest of high society and feted with balls and elaborate parties arranged by her mother. At the age of 17 the beautiful ingénue went off with a group of other well-to-do California girls to a Dresden finishing school where she was trained in the arts of *les grandes dames*. It was in Dresden that Amy fell in love with her first prince, Alexander of Saxe Weimar. Their relationship lasted a month. She then joined her mother for several months in Europe. They went to Madrid where Amy again fell in love, this time with a swarthy toreador who took her breath away and prompted her mother to whisk her off to London. It was there that she met David Kalakaua, the king of the Sandwich Islands (Hawaii), and spent hours listening to his stories about his home, an exotic paradise that sparked Amy's imagination and set the course of her life.

King Kalakaua of Hawaii (Library of Congress)

She returned to California and got her own apartment in San Francisco, where she fell in with the social set and pursued the course of most young, upper class women of the day, attending parties and parading the latest styles of clothing along the promenades of the city.

In February 1883 she and her mother traveled to Hawaii for the long-delayed official coronation of their friend King Kalakaua. It was a two-week long celebration in which the king showcased traditional Hawaiian arts like ukulele playing and the hula, which had earlier been banned as immodest at the insistence of Christian missionaries. The ban had not been lifted, but the king cared more about bringing back native Hawaiian culture than he did for the missionaries.

In Kalakaua, Amy had found a kindred spirit. Throughout her life she was disgusted by the disapproval and restriction of indigenous cultural practices imposed by her contemporaries around the globe. Wherever she traveled, it always gave her pleasure to cross the line and join in the local festivities, arousing alarm and condemnation from her fellow travelers, who, she knew, were not having nearly as much fun riding their high horses.

At eighteen Amy secretly married twenty-one year old San Franciscan R. Porter Ashe of Asheville, NC. Porter would later become the friend and guardian of Sarah Althea Hill Terry (Chapter VI). A story often told about Amy and her first marriage was that Porter Ashe and Harry Gillig played cards for her hand, Ashe winning with four aces. How true could it be? Four aces, after all! Nevertheless, Ashe was a big gambler, so the story naturally stuck. It was also a tidy tale because Amy went on to marry Gillig after divorcing Ashe.

Amy's mother gave the young Ashes a gift of a mansion on the corner of Washington and Van Ness in San Francisco. The couple soon had a daughter they named Gladys. Young Porter spent a lot of time at the racetrack and playing cards, losing a fortune on such pastimes. As a result, Amy took her daughter and left him, returning to her mother. When she and her mother went to San Francisco in 1887 to attend a wedding, Porter and his brother kidnapped little Gladys from her babysitter, starting a notorious scandal that ended in the courts with Amy's mother being granted legal custody of the baby.

Now free of both husband and child, Amy decided to go on an adventure. Not surprisingly, she settled on Hawaii as her first stop. She hired the *Tropic Star*, captained by Ephraim Judd, who agreed to put his vessel at her disposal so long as she was not a missionary. As if! She chartered the ship for a year and set sail for Honolulu. Upon her arrival, King Kalakaua offered her the choice of an American house (ordered from Sears Roebuck & Co.) or a room in the hotel. She took the house for a time, but later gave it up and moved into a typical Hawaiian grass hut.

In Hawaii, she spent her time riding horses, swimming, and dancing the hula, living like a native Hawaiian. Her behavior upset the missionaries who wanted her to behave like a white woman and set a standard for the natives to look up to. Both the king and Amy breezily dismissed these protests. The king gave Amy the gift of her own island near Molokai, setting her up as the island's monarch, and naming her Princess Palaikalani, which means "Bliss of Heaven." She remained good friends with the royal family of Hawaii for the remainder of Kalakaua's life.

From Hawaii, Amy and her crew sailed for Tahiti, then Samoa, visiting several Polynesian islands before she returned to California in 1889 and married Commodore Henry M. Gillig.

She next traveled to the Far East, sailing for Japan with her latest husband. He was called back to San Francisco for two months, but Amy remained in Japan and entered into a relationship with a wealthy local, Baron Takamini who showed her the real Japan, not the country normally experienced by Western visitors. In her memoirs, Amy makes reference to legendary Japanese tattoo artist Hori Chiyo, who was most likely responsible for at least one of her tattoos while she was in Japan. At the time, tattoos, especially for women, but even for men, were considered degrading and licentious, associated as they were by Europeans with so-called "uncivilized" people. For this reason, Amy took all the more pleasure in getting them.

Back in San Francisco, the Gilligs decided to divorce. As Amy put it, their life together was "not advisable."

Amy was now really free to follow her heart, and the path was becoming more and more clear to her. Off she went to China where she took a lover, an evil and powerful man with a habit of marrying wealthy young women then killing them. When Amy fled his house with the help of a servant, she narrowly escaped being slain by a carefully thrown knife. The servant, however, did not escape.

Having had enough of China, Amy then traveled to Singapore, Java, and Borneo where she met, yes, a man, though, of course, no ordinary man, but a native prince of Koetai, a tribe of head hunters who were adept at shooting poison darts with blowguns. Prince Djoet-ta whose English name was Joe, kidnapped Amy from her hotel and took her to his palace deep in the wilds of Borneo, intending to make her his wife. His father objected, however, and ordered his people to kill the interloper. Amy barely escaped yet again, launched into the river in a dugout canoe during the night. She floated down the river all the next day to the remote Dutch outpost of Long Iram where she was rescued, revived, and sent on her way.

Next she traveled to India, and it was there that she found what she had been looking for, the Eastern experience that touched her core. Not that there wasn't also a man in the equation. He was the Maharajah of Shikapur who became her guide. His good friend Bhurlana had a harem, which so fascinated Amy that she begged to live in the harem for a while to see what it was like. "He insisted that no woman but an Easterner could possibly adapt herself to the life," Amy wrote in her autobiography. "He even implied that I might be shocked. Naturally, that sealed the bargain."

Amy spent two weeks in the harem as Bhurlana's guest and observed the daily routine of the forty or so women. She attended banquets and watched the entertainment performed for the princes, including a snake dance with a cobra, her introduction to the art form that she would eventually adopt. Her experiences there were exciting, mysterious, romantic, spiritual, brutal, horrifying, and sometimes dangerous. She fell in love with India, both the ugliness and beauty, and never fell out of it. In her autobiography, she ended her tales of that country with the following sentiment: "Oh, India! Perhaps the years I spent in that never-to-be-understood land were the best of my life. I have told stories of people, but I never can tell the poetry, the rich beauty of it. It was the last strand of truly free adventure and romance in my life."

Amy would return to San Francisco or New York from time to time, but she continued her travels in Asia for ten years, collecting lovers, tattoos, and jewels, especially pearls, wherever she went. She also converted to Buddhism, a shocking development to many of her acquaintances.

In the 1890s, Amy had a home in Larchmont, New York, which she considered her permanent residence. Her mother Margaret decided to move there as well and bought property adjacent to her daughter's. Before moving to New York, she donated the family's art collection, along with the gallery building, to the city of Sacramento. The event was marked with an elaborate two-day flower festival to honor and celebrate Mrs. Crocker's generosity. The Crocker Art Gallery has remained an important Sacramento venue ever since. Today, the former Crocker Mansion is part of the museum.

Amy eventually ceased her Eastern travels, but the influences of those exotic lands became fully integrated into her social and domestic life. She often wore snakes around her neck at parties. She founded the first Buddhist colony in Manhattan, and it was there that she met her third husband, songwriter Jackson Gouraud. He was best known for "Waldorf-Hyphen-Astoria" (1899), a jaunty song describing how to behave at that famous establishment.

Amy's interest in tattoos did not diminish and it was shortly after she began her affair with Gouraud that she commissioned more ink in New York from one of Hori Chiyo's apprentices, Yoshisuke Hori Toyo. He adorned her arms with a demon's head, a Japanese beetle, and two snakes, one twisted to make the initials "A.G.," the other, the initials "J.G." Jackson Gouraud got the same snake tattoos to celebrate his love of Amy.

Amy divorced Gillig and married Gouraud in June 1901. Amy's daughter Gladys married Jackson Gouraud's brother, Powers Gouraud in 1903.

The Gourauds lived in Oriental-themed houses in New York and adopted four children and a few bulldogs. The Gouraud mansion in Larchmont was a constant source of curiosity, as its décor reflected the travels and interests of its mistress. A Sacramento reporter, granted a tour in 1909, observed:

> In her bedroom is a dark elephant bed with draperies of dark-blue silk and a Japanese dragon, gold in the center, and the windows are draped with five curtains of Oriental design and coloring, but the chief quality of strangeness of the room centers in the peculiar shrine erected beside her bed—the last thing she sees before going to sleep, the first to see when she wakes. A light burning in an orange globe and softened by a silken fringe of dark blue hangs above the shrine and never goes out. It is the whim of this American woman that she shall always be under the guiding eye of Buddha. In the shrine built into the wall this Buddha, bronze and naked except for a crown of rubies upon his brow, squats in everlasting silence and apparently everlasting vigilance. He is surrounded by a dozen other Buddhas, smaller ones, and at his crossed feet a bronze woman of dark, inscrutable face.[17]

In some sense, Amy followed in her mother's footsteps by hosting the most imaginative and poshest of parties, becoming a renowned hostess in San Francisco and New York as her mother had been in Sacramento. Among her guests and friends were Oscar Wilde, Enrico Caruso, the Barrymores, Diamond Jim Brady, and Lillian Russell. But Amy's parties were of a different flavor from those of her mother. The entertainment could be risqué; it was always exotic. On a winter's night in 1909, the Gourauds hosted a party at the Cafe Martin in New York that hit the newspapers back in San Francisco, a city always ready to claim Amy Crocker as a home town girl. The San Francisco *Call* reported: "In the gorgeous robes of the kaimur of Ghosh, the irrepressible Jackson Gouraud assisted his wife, splendidly gowned in green and gold with the jade ornamentation of an Egyptian queen, in receiving the gay throng that surged into the Fifth Avenue ballroom on the third floor of the restaurant."[18]

Amy was driven to create greater and greater spectacles to entertain her friends. To that end, she developed a dance program that became world famous. It was called "The Dance of all Nations," in which she danced routines from different cultures, some of them traditional, like "Salome" or an Argentinian tango, and some of them invented by Amy herself, like the Vienna "viggle" and Dogmeena the cannibal, in which she was covered with coconut oil and a red sash. Of course she included *La Danse de Cobra,* wearing a twelve-foot long snake, which she described as "gentle as a powder puff." An article in the November 21, 1911, *Sacramento Union* described the program as follows: "Tropical dances, tempestuous dances, dances filled with wild, weird tumult; slow, throbbing dances that turn the soul on its beam ends; danceless dances, suggesting the oriental, occult and devout; turkey trots and Honolulu 'Boola Boolas.'"

Amy wrote several short stories fashioned from her adventures, incorporating characters based on her many friends, thinly disguised. Some of these were published in a book titled *Moon-madness: And Other Fantasies.*

Jackson Gouraud, the love of Amy's life, died in 1910 of tonsillitis and blood poisoning. In that same year, an exotic dancer known as "The Maid of Mystery" appeared in a rooftop venue obscured in veils and "Oriental robes," performing an act not unlike the dance act Amy had often performed for her house guests. Though many guessed at the mysterious maid's identity, Amy denied that it was her.

In 1912 Amy left New York to make a permanent home in her favorite European city, Paris, where she bought a mansion for $150,000. Shortly thereafter, she had a room specially furnished with pillows and rugs and mother-of-pearl inlays for her new pet, a huge boa constrictor named Kaa, a gift from Princess Mara Davi, the daughter of an Indian Rajah.

It was during this time in Paris that Amy decided to put a French twist on her name and began spelling it Aimée.

Her fourth husband, taken in 1914, was Alexander Miskinoff, who dubbed himself "Prince," but was apparently of no royal lineage. "We Americans have a weakness for titles, real or not," Aimée observed. At least *she* certainly did.

It wasn't long before unrest occurred in this marriage. The prince hated the cobra dance, the mysticism of the Orient, and almost every other passion embraced by his wife. He complained that she had no interest in domestic life and spent too much time in cabarets. He also abhorred Aimée's short stories. This marriage was destined for divorce even before the shocking scandal that invaded it. Aimée's adopted daughter Yvonne fell in love with Miskinoff and he succumbed to her desires, pursuing an affair with the fifteen year old girl. Aimée sent the two of them away to live together, telling them that if they were still in love in a few months, she would divorce the prince and the two of them could marry. The girl soon tired of Miskinoff and left his bed. Aimée divorced him anyway. Several years later, she routinely claimed never to have been married to him at all, though there is a record of the marriage in London's St. Martins registry. She most likely *wished* she had never married him, however, and she continued to go by the name of Madame Gouraud.

In the spring of 1920 Aimée caused a sensation when she joined the fashionable promenaders along the Champs-Elysees in Paris wearing a jewelry store's worth of hardware. Among the beautiful and wealthy fashionistas of the day, Aimée turned heads and drew sufficient ahhs and oohs to make her feel triumphant. She attributed her success to her 48 million franc collection of pearls, pearls of every color and description, in elaborate settings and long strands. "My beautiful pearls," she murmured endearingly. "They made Paris stare at me. I could see looks of envy on the faces of women younger, more beautiful and better dressed than I was. I noticed admiration on every hand. My beautiful pearls!"[19] Aimée's collection of pearls became legendary, being by this time one of the largest and most impressive in the world. Her passion for them had begun when she was still a teenager and admired her mother's pearls best of all her jewelry. She associated pearls with Asia, and said "the soul of the Orient glows in the luster of pearls."

Although Aimée had quickly tired of Prince Miskinoff, she had thoroughly enjoyed being called "Princess." She regained that title at the age of 61 (she admitted to 51) when she married for the final time another Russian prince. Mistislav Galitzine was only 26 in 1925 when they married in Paris, but unlike his predecessor, he actually was a member of a venerated noble family. When asked if he was her fifth or sixth husband, Aimée replied, "The prince is my twelfth husband if I include in my matrimonial list seven Oriental husbands, not registered under the laws of the Occident."[20]

The couple sailed to New York soon after their wedding, staying in separate cabins. When they arrived, the society pages were all atwitter about the new husband and the new tattoos, a snake on her leg and a butterfly on her back. Two months later Aimée sailed back to Paris by herself. The following year, the marriage was over and she sued for a legal separation. During the court sessions, Galitzine claimed that Aimée had hired a friend to find her a true prince for a husband and Galitzine had agreed to the role, which included a stipend of $250 a month to play the part of her husband. The marriage was a sham, he said, designed to allow her to be a princess again, and the two of them were merely companions. In May 1927 Aimée was given a divorce, but she continued to use the name Princess Galitzine when it suited her. After her final marriage and divorce, Aimée was heard from less frequently. Her life became much quieter and more confined to New York.

In 1936 her autobiography was published to mixed reviews. Many thought it was lurid and a disgrace to the Crocker family name. Others thought it thrilling and fascinating, though written more like a fictional fantasy than real life. The following year, Aimée hired the Coleman Wise auction house to auction off $50,000 worth of her household possessions, described as "Oriental Art Treasures." Perhaps she needed the money.

On February 7, 1941, Aimée Crocker Ashe Gillig Gouraud Miskinoff Galitzine, aged 78, died of pneumonia in her Savoy-Plaza apartment. Her estate, worth over a million dollars, went to her daughter Gladys.

Aimée Crocker, the rich and eccentric heiress who devoted her life to living well, ended her autobiography with a quotation from an obscure poem by Fernand Gregh, which translates as follows:

> I have drunk my joy at the great sacred feast;
> What more do I want?
> I have lived,
>   And I will die.

Aimée Crocker (Crocker Art Museum)

IV. GENDER BENDERS

This chapter tells the stories of three unconventional individuals, different from one another, but all notorious for the same reason—they wore men's clothing.

In the mid-1800s, a spate of laws were passed in the United States making cross-dressing a crime. Anti-vagrancy laws were also used to prosecute cross-dressers, as in the New York statute of 1845, which stated that "Every person who, having his face painted, discolored, covered or concealed, or being otherwise disguised, in a manner calculated to prevent him from being identified, shall appear in any road or public highway, or in any field, lot, wood or enclosure, may be pursued and arrested." This law was used to arrest both men and women under the claim that wearing clothing of the opposite gender constituted a disguise.

Today, cross-dressing women are often assumed to fall somewhere on the LGBT+ spectrum of gender variance, but to make the same assumption about Gilded Age cross-dressers would be a mistake. There were lesbians then as now who wore men's clothing. But there were other reasons. The life of a woman in those days was remarkably different from those of modern women. They had extremely limited freedom to determine their own fates. Some women dressed in men's clothing because they wanted the freedom to make their own choices, the ability to get a non-traditional job, to travel safely, or even to be more comfortable. Harriet French, arrested in 1856 in New York for wearing men's clothing, told the press that she did it because she got paid more as a man. There were many reasons a woman might have dressed as a man, and not all of them involved sexual orientation.

Still, the practice was rare, so rare that whenever it occurred there was a hue and cry in the press and pulpit that generally took the form of condemnation. It may be hard for us to understand why a woman in pants was such a big deal to nineteenth-century America. To fully understand the objection, we have to consider what else was happening during this historical era. It was a critical time for women's rights, a period referred to as the First Wave of feminism or the Suffrage Movement, which officially began with the 1848 Women's Rights Convention in Seneca Falls, New York, and ended with the adoption of the 19th Amendment to the Constitution in 1920.

Anti-suffragist poster of 1913 (Univ. of Wisconsin Library)

Throughout this time, women activists spoke out and marched across the nation for equal rights, primarily the right to vote, but also the right to own property, to execute legal documents, to earn equal pay, to have legal custody of their children, and many other rights that many women take for granted today. These protestors advanced the concept of "The New Woman," a woman who was not simply the appendage of her husband, but was capable of independent thought and deserved to be treated as an autonomous being.

One of the most common arguments against giving women the right to vote was that they would obviously vote the same as their husbands, so there was no point. The voices of unmarried women were not considered of any importance.

This was the context behind the fear and outrage that accompanied a woman wearing trousers in the latter half of the nineteenth and early twentieth centuries. Cross-dressing was associated with the danger of feminism, which many believed was an attempt to undermine the natural order and topple the patriarchy. Wearing men's clothing was often seen as an abomination against God, which is exactly the argument that many people made against women's rights in general, or, for that matter, the civil rights of Native Americans, African Americans, homosexuals, and other oppressed groups. Women's suffrage was a topic constantly in the news during the Gilded Age, and it caused intense anger on both sides. The campaign against women's rights was primarily one of fearmongering, warning good Americans that if women were allowed to vote, the fabric of society would completely unravel. It was a highly polarizing social and political issue like so many issues facing us today. So, perhaps, given this context, we can understand why cross-dressing women raised a few hackles, even if their motives had nothing to do with politics.

It took over 70 years of organized, nationwide campaigning for women to get the vote, which wasn't aided by the fact that all legislation was thoroughly controlled by male legislators and voters. It was a long and arduous struggle for generations of feminists and feminist sympathizers to win just this one legal right, and, as with all such civil rights struggles, incremental victories have been achieved over time, but total victory remains elusive.

After 1920, therefore, women could legally vote, but wearing pants was still mostly frowned upon. Laws against cross-dressing continued to be passed in the U.S. as late as the 1950s, though by then women were wearing pants in increasing numbers. This fashion movement was pioneered by unapologetic actresses like Marlene Dietrich and Katharine Hepburn who rocked trousers when most ordinary housewives wouldn't have dared to appear in public in them.

For younger readers, keep in mind that up until 1972 when the Title IX non-discrimination provisions were passed in the U.S., girls were required to wear dresses in school, so this type of clothing restriction has had a long history.

Marlene Dietrich in 1933

When it suited society for women to wear men's clothing, such as during WWII when women went to work in factories, then women could do so, but for the most part, prior to the 1970s, it did not suit society to allow it. The women who did so could expect to be harassed, persecuted, arrested, even imprisoned or confined to a mental institution. It is no surprise, then, that two of the three subjects in this chapter made a decision to keep their biological gender a lifelong secret. By doing so, they gained the ability to live as they wished and avoid the intolerance of society. But living with such a secret often comes at a cost in terms of personal happiness. Although there have been a few cases of Victorian-era transgender people being married and raising families, for the most part, an individual disguising his or her biological gender in this time period led a solitary and wary life.

Thankfully, women in trousers is no longer a crime or even an aberration, and nobody thinks anything of it. Like the old Virginia Slims commercials said, "You've come a long way, baby."

CHARLEY PARKHURST (1812 – 1879)
"One-Eyed Charley"

Charley Parkhurst

Charley Parkhurst was a legendary stagecoach driver or "whip," as they were known, in early California. The job was dangerous and physically demanding. Handling a team of up to six horses on rough roads frequented by highwaymen required skill, daring, and a cool head. Charley was renowned as one of the best among a scant handful of mythical stage drivers. The others were Hank Monk (mentioned in a humorous tale in Mark Twain's *Roughing It*), Clark Foss, and Bill Spiers.

If you were a stage driver, you took a few knocks along the way. You could lose an eye, like Charley did, with a kick from a frisky horse, or you could have your life threatened by rolling the stage or facing the gun of an outlaw, both of which happened to Charley more than once. During one of those times when the coach went out of control and rolled over, there were fortunately no passengers on board, but Charley sustained several blows, bruises, and a few broken ribs, but did not seek medical attention. Was Charley just that resilient, or was the tough-as-nails coach driver afraid of doctors? The latter was certainly true, for Charley had a secret that a doctor's examination could easily uncover. That chaw chewing, one-eyed codger was not the man people thought they knew. Charley was not a man at all, but he had spent nearly all of his life under this guise, keeping the secret, as far as anybody knows, from absolutely everyone he met.

Charlotte Durkee Parkhurst, the story goes, was born in New Hampshire around 1812. She was orphaned very young and raised in an orphanage until she ran away, dressed in boy's clothing, and met the owner of a livery stable, Ebenezer Balch, who apparently thought the girl was a boy and took Charley home to Providence, Rhode Island, to raise as his son. Balch taught Charley to drive a stagecoach and ride and care for horses.

This is one version of Charley's childhood. There are several. It's often said that nature abhors a vacuum, and it follows that humans abhor a story without a beginning. Sometimes, however, there's simply no surviving information. Storytellers are tempted to reach, to add dots to the picture in order to connect them. There's reason to suspect that the origin story chosen here is mere speculation, but it is the one most often told, and once told, these stories gain credence by being repeated. There are no records, however, to tell us Charley's original name, biological parents, or what occurred during the first thirty years of Charley's life. There were no individuals who came forward during or after Charley's death to fill in the blanks. There was no confidante who had the answers, or if there was such a person, he or she never went public. The name Charlotte itself appears to be an invention. Since Charley self-identified as a male from the first known verifiable records of his life, male pronouns will be used in this account.

New Hampshire was likely his birthplace based on subsequent census records. Beyond that, little is certain, other than he knew how to handle a team of horses from a young age, and that by the age of thirty, he was living full time as a man, and likely had been doing so for a while.

In his thirties, Charley drove a hack, a horse-drawn taxi, for stable owner Charles H. Childs in Providence, Rhode Island. He lived in a boarding house owned by Hezekiah Allen, a fact backed up by the 1850 census and the recollections of a man who had known him during that time, B. P. Moore. "He had a strained, squeaking falsetto voice," he recalled, "and could swear the best of anything. He was quite a favorite among the boys about the stable and, indeed, his employer had the greatest confidence in him."[21]

While Charley was working in Rhode Island, news from the California Gold Rush swept through the East Coast, calling out to adventurous souls looking for opportunities. Though Charley was already thirty-nine, he answered the call and boarded a ship in Boston to travel to Panama, which he walked through to catch another ship to California. In Panama, he met John Morton who owned a drayage business in San Francisco. Morton hired Charley before they left Panama.

A few years later, he went to work for James E. Birch, another Rhode Island immigrant who founded the California Stage Company, the preeminent company operating in California at that time. Driving a hack in an Eastern city was an entirely different thing from driving a stage coach between mining camps in California, but Charley was up for the challenge.

During his time with Birch, Charley developed a reputation as one of the best whips on the West Coast. At that time there were no railroads in California, so the coaches were the standard means of travel between towns, and they also transported the mail.

Charley drove several routes through Central California. He had the Stockton to Mariposa route, Sacramento to Watsonville, San Jose to Oakland, and San Juan to Santa Cruz. Sometimes he even drove the Santa Cruz run both ways in one day, coming back by night to earn double the pay.

There are no known photographs of Charley, only a couple of sketches and some descriptions by people who met him. From these scraps we can put together a fair portrayal. Stage drivers usually wore a long, linen duster, a light overcoat, a wide brimmed hat, gloves, and tall leather boots.

IV. GENDER BENDERS

Charley favored a gray hat and hand-embroidered buckskin gloves. He also sported a black eyepatch over his blind left eye, which earned him the nickname "One-Eyed Charley." None who described his looks gave him high marks for attractiveness. More often they said he was a little hard to look at, with mottled skin and deep-cut lines on his pale face, "with now and then a hair that he pretended was a mustache." Charley was short and chunky with wide hips and a strange waddling gait. Personality-wise, he was quiet and rarely smiled. He was polite and companionable, but never got too chummy with anybody. On the road he often slept with the horses rather than bedding down with the men. When he was teased about that, he said he got along better with horses than people.

The stereotype of the whips of the west was that they were profane alcoholic, tobacco-spitting roughnecks, for, it was said, it took cursing to handle horses and whiskey to clear a throat clogged with dust. Charley did swear and did drink, but he never let booze interfere with his profession. In particular he excelled in the handling of his whip, and was routinely pleased to demonstrate his ability by cutting a cigar from a man's mouth at twenty feet.

"In the old stage days," related Ed Martin, a Santa Cruz resident who knew Charley well, "a seat by the driver was considered the post of honor, and was eagerly sought for by the traveler. One had a better view from the seat, at least it was supposed so, and came as it were into confidential relations with the driver; had the satisfaction of hearing the driver's experience over mountain roads, the hair-breadth escapes, anecdotes of distinguished men who sat on the box with him and whom he had entertained. The driver of the days of stage traveling was a very important personage."[22]

In June of 1858 the bandit known as Sugarfoot, named for his habit of wrapping burlap around his feet instead of wearing boots, held up Charley's stage on the Stockton to Mariposa route and ordered the driver to "throw down the box." Charley had been told to avoid a confrontation with thieves when possible. He handed the strongbox over to Sugarfoot, but the incident left a foul taste in his mouth. He was determined not to be taken advantage of a second time. Sugarfoot and his gang held him up again on the same route six months later. This time Charley was ready. He let loose the horses, who plowed through the bandits, and let loose the guns, wounding one of Sugarfoot's men. He also wounded and inflicted fatal shots on the infamous outlaw himself. Sugarfoot dragged himself to a miner's cabin and died of his wounds. Charley had a reputation after that among outlaws as a dangerous mark.

Charley Parkhurst (left) and journalist J. Ross Bown
(*Harper's Monthly*, 1865)

In 1867 fifty-five year old Charley applied to join the Odd Fellows Lodge in Soquel and was accepted. He maintained his membership there for the remainder of his life. That same year he registered to vote, making Charley the first woman in California to vote for president.

By this time, Charley was well known and well respected, but he was getting older and slowing down. The hard work was taking a toll. "I've driven stages nigh on to 30 years," he told a newspaper reporter. "I'm no better off than when I commenced; pay's small; work heavy; getting rheumatism in the bones; nobody to look out for used-up old stage drivers."[23]

Once the railroads came to California, driving a stage coach was no longer as profitable and the routes were further off the main lines, so Charley retired from the stage business and settled down to farming in the summer and lumbering in the winter in the area of Watsonville. He could swing an ax with the best of them and never shied away from the heaviest labor. Charley was level-headed and thrifty, not prone to throwing money around, and he was able to save several thousand dollars from his wages. He lived simply and had few possessions. The one thing he'd always carried with him, though, was a small tin trunk that was always locked.

While he was logging in the Santa Cruz mountains, he boarded with Andy Jackson Clark in Hungry Hollow. One night Charley came home dead drunk and Mrs. Clark told her teenage son to help him to bed. A few minutes later, the boy ran back with the astonishing declaration that Charley wasn't a man, but a woman. This was perhaps the only time that Charley's secret was revealed. The Clarks were respectful, however, and decided not to share what they had discovered. There were others who later came forward to say that they had long suspected Charley of being a woman, but they had never pressed the issue and had respected Charley's privacy.

As Charley aged, he decided to give up the physically demanding occupations of his younger years and opened a horse-changing station and saloon on the old Santa Cruz Road between Santa Cruz and Watsonville. He was able to buy a cattle ranch with his savings. When his neighbor, a widow with a daughter, went bankrupt and had her land foreclosed on, out of sympathy, Charley bought the place in the auction and gave it back to the widow, no strings attached.

He suffered severely from rheumatoid arthritis and in his declining years was forced to retire altogether. He sold the saloon and ranch and moved into a small cabin at Moss Ranch about six miles from Watsonville. In his sixties, Charley contracted cancer of the mouth and throat.

Frank Woodward was a friend of Charley's for twenty years. He was the one who stayed by his side during his last illness.

Charley died on December 18, 1879, at the age of 67, and it was when his body was being prepared for burial that his long-held secret became public. The doctor reported that not only was Charley a woman, but at some time had given birth to a child. In Charley's locked tin trunk were discovered a small red dress and a pair of baby shoes. What happened to the child remains a mystery.

The revelation of Charley's gender created a sensation and ensured his enduring notoriety. Frank Woodward felt betrayed, as he had been so loyal a friend and Charley hadn't trusted him with the truth. Others took the news more jovially, like Hank Monk, himself a celebrated and storied whip from the old days. "Je-hosaphat!" he exclaimed. "I camped out with Parkie once for over a week and we slept on the same buffalo robe right along; wonder if Curley Bill's playing me the same way."[24]

No relatives or potential heirs ever showed up to stake a claim on the estate, despite the fact that the story of Charley Parkhurst made national news. He was buried with full Odd Fellows honors by the Soquel Lodge in the old cemetery at 44 Main Street, Watsonville, now known as the Pioneer Cemetery.

In his will, he left $600 to a twelve year old neighbor boy, George Harmon, and other money to those who had cared for and been kind to him at the end of his life. It was rumored that Charley had buried a treasure somewhere, as there wasn't much money in the bank and he was known to have made quite a bit of money in the sale of his property. In 1891, many years after Charley's death, somebody dug a deep hole in the floor of a stable Charley had owned on San Vicente Creek.

IV. GENDER BENDERS

Did they find the treasure? Nobody knows. Maybe it's never been found.

In 1955 the Pajaro Valley Historical Association erected a monument to Charley in the Pioneer Cemetery. The inscription reads: Noted whip of the Gold Rush days drove stage over Mt. Madonna in early days of valley. Last run San Juan to Santa Cruz. Death in cabin near the 7 Mile House. Revealed 'One-Eyed Charley' a woman. The first woman to vote in the U.S., Nov. 3, 1868."

Charley was not the first woman to vote in the U.S., but was the first in California. There's a bronze plaque at the Soquel fire station where Charley voted, commemorating the history-making event.

Charley's legacy remains strong. Every few years the local papers resurrect the story for new readers, and it continues to be remembered and retold to this day. About nine years after his death, the Santa Cruz *Sentinel* ran a long story about Charley that contained this sentiment: "Parkhurst, the dashing driver, the fearless fighter of highwaymen, the strong lumberman, passed out of existence, and in his place was found something gentler and more tender…With astonishment at a deception so marvelously carried out comes the sad thought of all she must have suffered."[25]

No doubt Charley had suffered. There are the melancholy contents of the tin trunk, for one thing. And by necessity, Charley's life was a lonely one. Keeping a secret always takes an emotional toll. He led a life of physical hardship, incurring who knows how many injuries. He was described as walking with a limp, he'd lost an eye, he had seriously aggravated rheumatoid arthritis and cancer, and yet he never went to a doctor. There must have been a lot of pain, emotional and physical. On the other hand, he led an extremely adventurous and interesting life on the California frontier. He participated in the action in a way he could never have done living as a woman. And it was his choice to do so. He lived his truth, which is not a sad state of being. His life is therefore not to be pitied, but celebrated.

JEANNE BONNET (1849 - 1876)
"The Little Frog-Catcher"

Jeanne Bonnet

To prepare the French delicacy *cuisses de grenouille*, dredge freshly caught frog legs in flour, sauté them in butter and garlic, then dress with parsley and lemon. Voila! This was a taste of home to homesick French immigrants in 1850s California. Masses of frog legs were needed because 30,000 French men and women of all backgrounds and classes made the journey to San Francisco between 1849 and 1856, more than any other national group of fortune seekers. A wild fever swept through France with the beginning of the Gold Rush,

IV. GENDER BENDERS

and thousands paid the 1,000 francs to make the dangerous months-long journey. But even those who hadn't a sou got a chance at a new life. From 1851 to 1853 the French government held the "Lottery of the Golden Ingots" to pay the passage of 4,000 of its less desirable citizens. Among them were dissidents, criminals, and prostitutes. There were also honest, hard-working people who were simply scraping the bottom of their barrels. Into this category fell the family of Sosthène and Désirée Bonnet of Paris. They were actors who performed primarily at the Theatre Historique, which had to shutter its doors in 1851, leaving the Bonnets with no means of earning a living. They packed up their three-year old daughter Jeanne and booked passage to "The Paris of the West," San Francisco, where, they had heard, entertainers were treated like royalty and paid in gold nuggets. They sailed through the Golden Gate in 1852 and resumed their career, appearing regularly at the Metropolitan Theater. When she was old enough, Jeanne appeared on stage alongside her parents. Though they did not get rich, the Bonnets were popular and made a decent living.

In 1856 they welcomed another daughter, Blanche, into the family.

As a teenager, Jeanne was willful and free-spirited with a stubbornly individual streak that got her into plenty of trouble. She frequently got drunk and got into fights, and supplemented her allowance by shoplifting. As a result, she was committed to the Industrial School, San Francisco's first reform school (now the site of City College), at the age of fifteen.

Once released from the reformatory, Jeanne had few options. As a destitute, homeless young woman, like so many other French girls in San Francisco, she resorted to selling her body to survive. She was so desperately unhappy during this period that she tried to kill herself at the age of 23 by overdosing on laudanum. The incident was reported in the *Chronicle* as follows: "Jeanne Bonnet, a French woman of ill-fame, last evening made an attempt to end her existence by taking laudanum. She has for some time past been living with a man at No. 930 Kearny Street. Last night, about 9 o'clock, her paramour, on reaching the house, heard groans proceeding from the bedroom. Going inside he discovered that she was breathing very heavily and acting as if in great pain. He ran out and notified Dr. Johnson, who found that she had taken laudanum. Restoratives were applied, and about an hour afterward she was resting quite easy."[26]

Although the newspaper termed her companion her "paramour," he might also have been her pimp or, in French circles, her *maque*, a Frenchman who took half of his woman's earnings and provided her with physical protection when required.

Around 1873 Jeanne's mother died and her father retired from acting and moved to Oakland to find other types of work.

By the following year, Jeanne had transformed herself. She was no longer living with a man and was no longer working as a prostitute. Instead, she was herding sheep on a ranch in San Mateo. She cut her hair short, wore boys' clothing, and committed bold acts of thievery to help support herself. She was arrested numerous times, for burglary, for drinking in saloons (not allowed for women), and most often for wearing men's clothing, which was a crime. In court, her defense was that she had to wear such clothes to do her job.

By the summer of that same year, when Jeanne was twenty-five, she had found a new gig—frog catching in the ponds around Lake Merced. She was able to make good money selling these to the numerous French restaurants in the city. Jeanne quickly became well known around town because she was the only female frog catcher and because she wore men's clothing, which made her eccentric enough to attract attention. However, not everyone she dealt with knew she was a woman. Because of her clothing, some thought she was a boy and referred to her as the "little frog catcher." "She was called little," wrote W. C. Morrow in his feature story of her life, "because for a man she was small; for a woman she was of medium height, strong but slender. Her brown hair slightly curly, was kept closely cropped; her face was tanned brown by the sun; her dark gray eyes had a steady penetrating glance, in which there was a mixture of hardness and kindness. Her general appearance was that of an exceedingly wise, shrewd and independent lad who had grown to be a man before ceasing to be boy. Her hands were small, but brown with tan and hardened by the basket. In her dress she was careless, for her work would not permit neatness. For trousers she commonly wore overalls; above these a shirt of dark wool and a rough sack coat; a boy's shoes and a boy's black woolen hat completed her outfit."[27]

Jeanne was arrested numerous times for "promenading the streets in pantaloons." On one of these occasions in the summer of 1874 her lawyer argued that she couldn't do her job in a long skirt. He promised the judge that in the future, she would change out of her work clothes before walking around town. She was fined $10 and sent on her way, but she did not keep the promise. Only three weeks later she was again arrested and fined $20 for the same offense. By the following year, the fines she paid were nearing $100, but she refused to wear women's clothing, whether while mucking around at lakeside or patronizing bars and hotels. In fact, she even began wearing men's clothing to her court appearances, showing up in July 1876 as described by the *Morning Call* wearing "gray pantaloons, coat, vest, white shirt and a small, jaunty black hat." She had become well known by then and was referred to as the "girl frog catcher" and the "French girl-boy" in the press.

Jeanne was undeterred by fines, jail time, or any other difficulties her cross-dressing caused her. "The police might arrest me as often as they wish," she said defiantly, "I will never discard male attire for as long as I live."

Jeanne spent a lot of time with the police and the courts from 1874 through 1876. She was arrested often for wearing pants, but she was also arrested for excessive drinking on at least one occasion.

Meanwhile, her nineteen year old sister Blanche had become pregnant and was extremely depressed. She threatened suicide and begged people to kill her. As a result, she was declared insane by a probate judge and sent to the Stockton State Hospital on August 25, 1875. According to the hospital records, Blanche gave birth "to a male child Oct 16th 1875. Child died October 22nd 1875." Blanche was pronounced cured in 1878 and was discharged into the care of Charles and Jennie Douillard of Stockton. There's no evidence to suggest that Jeanne did or didn't have any contact with her sister during these years, but it seems likely that she was estranged from her family from her teens onward.

In her twenties, Jeanne began a crusade to liberate fallen women (primarily French ones) from their oppressors, their *maques*, just as she had liberated herself. She persuaded them to leave the men, leave the business, go out on their own, and help one another live free. Though Jeanne had little of her own, and was living on the streets much of the time, she helped these women in any way she could to get money, food, jobs, and to evade their former *maques*. Her efforts to vanquish prostitution gained her both enemies and friends. The *maques*, of course, hated and threatened her, which prompted her to carry a Colt revolver at all times. On the other hand, she was described in glowing terms by one reporter who, although acknowledging her less angelic side and her "peculiar" eccentricities, praised her for her war against pimps, which he vividly denounced. "They continue to flourish on the proceeds of iniquity, and each Saturday afternoon beholds them resplendent in bogus diamonds and waxed moustaches, prowling on the pavement of Kearny Street, and watching with furtive, cat-like glances for every opportunity to ply their nefarious business." [28]

There are stories that surfaced after Jeanne's death when she had become a mythic figure that describe her as the leader of a gang of former prostitutes that committed daring acts of thievery in the vein of Robin Hood, but there is no reason to believe these tales. It wasn't above Jeanne to steal, and no doubt that was part of her money-making strategy, but there are no accounts from the day that support the story of her running a merry band of fallen women.

One of the prostitutes Jeanne befriended was fellow French woman Blanche Beunon, who arrived in San Francisco in 1875 with her lover Arthur Deneve. The couple lived off her earnings as a prostitute. Deneve resented Blanche's friendship with Jeanne and forbade her from seeing her. But the bond between the two women only deepened and Jeanne persuaded Blanche to leave Deneve, which she did. A bitter Deneve, who claimed Blanche had pawned all his possessions and stolen all his money, left for the East Coast with funds from his sympathetic friends. His plan was to travel to Havana and join a troupe of performers.

With Deneve out of the way, the friends felt like celebrating. A few days after he left, on Tuesday, September 12, 1876, Jeanne and Blanche hired a wagon and drove to one of Jeanne's favorite hangouts, McNamara's Saloon at San Miguel Station (now Ocean View), for a couple days of togetherness. On Thursday evening the two women prepared for bed. After undressing, twenty-seven year old Jeanne reclined in bed and Blanche sat on the edge of it unlacing her shoe. An unseen assailant fired a shotgun through the window, hitting Jeanne with six shots. She cried out that she was hit and died immediately after.

Jeanne's funeral, a bleak affair held at the morgue, was attended largely by prostitutes and former prostitutes. She was buried at the Odd Fellow Cemetery, but in the 1930s her body was transferred to the Greenlawn Memorial Park in Colma, California, along with thousands of other remains that were relocated.

Jeanne was survived by her father, a diminished man who served drinks and swept floors in Leon Samson's saloon in Oakland. By 1880, however, Sosthène Bonnet, then 55, was incapacitated by partial paralysis and became dependent on Samson and his wife. He dropped out of the public eye except for his reappearance each year at the Bastille Day celebrations in San Francisco, where he sang a song or recited a poem to contribute to the festivities. Jeanne's sister Blanche remained in the home of Charles Douillard, acting as a family servant. Blanche Beunon died in 1877 of throat cancer.

The murder of a homeless woman didn't normally get much press, but Jeanne was already something of a legend at the time she died, and the public was tremendously interested in knowing all the details of her death. At first police assumed the murder was carried out by one of the angry pimps or a friend of Arthur Deneve, Ernest Gerard, who had unsuccessfully intervened on Deneve's behalf to break up the two women. Gerard was arrested, but released when he produced a sound alibi. Though interest in the case remained high, no evidence could be found to make an arrest and the case went cold, becoming known as "The Mystery of San Miguel."

Four years later the case was reopened when a man named Lewis Duffranant brutally assaulted his wife Caroline at their Canadian home. Caroline, being moved to rat on her husband, told authorities that he was the murderer of Jeanne Bonnet, that he had gone to the saloon that night to kill Blanche Beunon, but when she had leaned down to undo her shoe, the shot had missed her, hitting Jeanne instead. The San Francisco police persisted for some time in the case against Duffranant, taking a detailed statement from his wife, which helped them piece together the events of that fatal night. Years earlier Duffranant was an innkeeper at San Miguel Station under the name Pierre Louis. A witness was found who claimed that Louis/Duffranant took money to kill Blanche Beunon. Duffranant was eventually taken into custody in Canada. Before he could be extradited, however, he hung himself.

So ends the story of the little frog catcher who captured the attention and fired the imaginations of generations of Californians with her bravado and fierce independence. Her fascinating life could easily have been the subject of a major motion picture, but, sadly, the ending of such a film would be too disappointing. A cowardly, unseen assailant fires into the bedroom of his victim, misses her and inadvertently kills the noble thief, then runs away in the night. Not a hero's death by any means.

ELVIRA VIRGINIA MUGARRIETA (1869 – 1936)
"Uncle Jack"

Jack Bee Garland, 1897 (photo by Ed McCullagh)

On September 18, 1936, a short, diminutive man with iron gray hair walked to the corner of Post and Franklin Streets in San Francisco, his gait inhibited by debilitating abdominal pain. The condition had been troubling him for several days, steadily worsening. Now his illness overtook him and he collapsed on the sidewalk. Passersby called an ambulance and the man was taken to the hospital to be treated for acute peritonitis. Papers on his person identified him as sixty-six year old Jack Bee Garland, a San Francisco resident. However, the attending medical staff soon discovered that their patient was not a man after all, but a woman in men's clothing. The patient died on September 20 and the incident was widely reported in the newspapers. Known to locals as a kind, self-styled social worker who tended to the homeless men of the city, "Uncle Jack" as he was called, was familiar to many. But his secret had been well kept for decades, and the news that he was born female was a shock to those who depended on his kindness. Within a few days of his death, Jack's life story was revealed by his one living relative, his sister Victoria, who came forward to say that Jack Bee Garland was actually her sister Elvira.

Elvira Virginia Mugarrieta was born in San Francisco on December 9, 1869, to José Marcos Mugarrieta, a distinguished Mexican military officer and Eliza Alice Garland Mugarrieta, a Maryland-born daughter of a state supreme court justice. José Mugarrieta, who had served as the secretary to the Mexican Minister of War and personal aide to President Arista, was sent to California in 1859 to establish the first Mexican consulate in San Francisco, and he soon became a well-respected and prominent figure in the city. He was removed from that position in 1863 after he refused to help General Plácido Vega obtain weapons and ammunition from the U.S., an act that would have been illegal during the Civil War. The family remained in San Francisco, where Mugarrieta earned a living as a Spanish teacher and translator. The family finances were greatly reduced as a result.

Elvira developed a wanderlust early and reveled in listening to tales of other people's travels. "Oh, if I were but a boy!" she wrote. "Just to be able to see all these beautiful things!"

A willful and tomboyish girl, she worried her mother, who decided to send her to a convent school where she would receive strict instruction and perpetual supervision. Unable to leave the school, Elvira grew sad and felt her lack of freedom keenly. Her brother William visited often at first, bringing along a friend, but eventually he came less frequently. After William quit visiting his sister, the friend continued. She described him as "a rather quiet, unassuming sort of a chap." When she was released for the holidays during her fifteenth year, she sought out the boy and told him that she couldn't bear her life of confinement anymore. She needed to escape and see the world. She hatched a plan that they should be married and then she would be free. The young man agreed and the two of them went away together. It was a short-lived union. They divorced after a few weeks and Elvira returned home to find her family, especially her mother, extremely disappointed in her.

On June 14, 1886, José Mugarrieta died. Sixteen year old Elvira was deeply affected by the loss. She had been much closer to her father than her mother and felt his absence deeply. "From a tomboy full of ambitions," she later wrote, "I was made into a sad and thoughtful woman. From that time I grew heartless. I wanted to be out in the air always. A desire for liberty and freedom took such a hold upon me that at night, when all were asleep, I would get up and wander about our immediate grounds as if in search of something I could not tell what."

Before long, Elvira's mother gave up trying to turn her into a respectable young woman and set her free, sending her off with an allowance. The young woman entered a period of intense loneliness. "From that moment," she wrote, "I have been like driftwood tossed upon the sea of life." To protect herself, she dressed as a boy and wandered through California, roaming in the Santa Cruz mountains and the Sierras, visiting both tiny towns and major cities and camping for weeks at a time under the stars.

While Elvira had become a vagabond, her brother William had turned to a life of crime, committing thefts and burglaries in Sacramento and San Francisco. By 1896 he was incarcerated in San Quentin and in ill health. His mother and sisters did what they could to have him released and finally succeeded in obtaining a pardon from the governor in March 1896 when it became clear that William wouldn't survive much longer. His mother hired a hack to meet him at the ferry dock in Sausalito where he launched into a coughing fit and began hemorrhaging blood from his mouth. When he recovered, the family took him home where he died a month later.

After a brief stay with her family, Elvira's solitary adventures continued, and on July 14, 1897, she walked into the Central Valley city of Stockton, CA, where she took up residence on a houseboat (termed an "ark" by residents) in McLeod Lake, assuming the name Babe Bean. From the day of her arrival in Stockton, she didn't speak a word to anyone, and conducted all of her communication in writing, claiming she was mute and had lost her voice during "a fit of anger" many years earlier.

Complaints of a woman masquerading about town as a man began to come into the police department, and the police kept their eyes out for the culprit. About a month after her arrival, Elvira was apprehended as she walked to a church to listen to a concert.

She responded to questioning in a written statement in which she identified herself as a woman and said that she wore men's clothes for safety as she traveled alone, and she had found that it was much easier to get work as a man. She convinced them that she had no nefarious motives in dressing as she did. Now 27, Elvira gave her age as only 20 and described a hard luck story that had led to her wandering the land in near destitution. The police could tell from her writing that she was a woman of breeding, which went a long way in gaining their sympathy. They concluded that she was harmless, and released her without punishment.

Several area newspapers carried the story of the betrousered mystery woman. The *San Francisco Call* wrote, "Babe Bean has the dark hair and full mouth that tell of love of music, adventure and pleasure." The *Call* was so captivated by this curious young woman that they published a longer article about her a few days after the police business entitled "Story of a Modern Rosalind," recalling the cross-dressing heroine of Shakespeare's *As You Like It*. When the reporter suggested to her that he believed she could actually talk, she burst into tears and declared (on paper) that she wished she could, that she was deeply depressed by her lack of speech. Because of Babe's affliction, the session with the reporter took the form of a written history of her life. Babe was an excellent writer and the newspaper published her story exactly as she had written it.

After coming to the attention of the press, poor Babe was shadowed by journalists constantly. They reported her every move, trying to unravel the mystery of her true gender and her ability or lack of ability to speak, both issues being still in question by the press. Her neighbors who also lived on boats in the lake were questioned daily about her movements. It was reported that she had a companion named Rodell, that she went out one evening with a man and did not come back, that her boat remained dark all night on that occasion, and even in the morning she wasn't there. On another evening she went to the theater, sat in the gallery, smoked a cigarette on her walk home, and met a friend there. A couple of days later she attempted to hop off a moving streetcar and was dashed to the ground, getting knocked unconscious. She was treated for a bad bump to the forehead and remained home for a couple of days to recuperate. All of these details were carefully reported by the local papers, down to describing her clothes (dark trousers, red sweater, and white cap) and what she liked to drink when out on the town (soda water). It seemed the good people of Stockton could not get enough of the odd newcomer. The local Bachelor Club even named her an honorary member, which pleased her greatly. Babe was clearly delighted to move freely through the world of men.

A longshoreman riding on the same streetcar that caused Babe's accident overheard her say that her encounter with the pavement hurt like hell. He also claimed to know Mr. Rodell, Babe's friend, who had told him that the mute act was just that, an act.

Despite the discomfort of her first few months in town, Babe Bean remained in Stockton and made herself a part of the community, writing opinion pieces for the local paper, frequenting civic events, even playing her guitar at public recitals. She had charmed the police, who decided there was no harm in her, and she found defenders among the editors of the *Stockton Evening Mail*. The city, for the most part, accepted her eccentricities with good humor. That wasn't always true in other places and times, and at least twice in her life, Babe was arrested for wearing men's clothing, though she was never convicted of a crime. So it's not surprising she stayed in Stockton. She found the cultural stimulation she craved, especially music, and she was able to live as she pleased.

Babe's *Stockton Evening Mail* articles reveal a paradoxical point of view. Although her personal habits and lifestyle were unorthodox, her beliefs were not, at least as she expressed them in writing. She opposed women's suffrage, preferring traditional roles for women. She generally praised men, especially those in power, and criticized women, especially feminists. "No. No new woman for me," she wrote, responding to a question asked of all public female figures of the time about their stance on women's rights. It was clear from this sort of statement that at this time Babe freely acknowledged her female gender while disavowing feminist doctrine, leading most of the men in town to accept her as nonthreatening. She was not a woman trying to overthrow the patriarchy, they concluded, just a quirky girl in pants. She refused all invitations from society women, had no female friends, and was generally dismissive of women, stating that she preferred the company of men.

Babe's letters to the editor were so well received that the *Evening Mail* put her on the payroll. Her first official assignment was to cover a baby contest at the San Joaquin County Fair. Along with detailed descriptions of the newborn participants, Babe also defended the right of a black woman to enter her child in the contest. This was the sort of assignment that might be given to any female reporter, but Babe's interests trended more toward investigative reporting. The following day, she turned in an exposé of the cheating she had observed in men's keno joints, something no other woman would be privy to. The article led to a city ordinance banning keno. Babe could be seen walking around town at all hours of the night, delving into areas that women were normally not allowed, exposing vice and crime and social problems, gaining the confidence of hobos, grifters, and gamblers by posing as a man.

IV. GENDER BENDERS

One evening she posed as a runaway boy and settled into a hobo camp on the shore of McLoed Lake, writing a story about the tramp life she found there, an existence that clearly intrigued her. She also wrote about the culture she found among the permanent residents of McLoed Lake. "Instead of conforming to the general way of living," she wrote, "most of the ark-dwellers that I have noticed live a happy-go-lucky sort of an existence. No home can be more modest; no life more free….As yet I have heard no cries of lamentation, of mourning nor weeping, notwithstanding the majority of my neighbors have seen better days."

She gained the friendship and support of local government officials and the police, who seemed to put her into a category all her own where gender conforming laws did not apply. Because of this, the women in town who were actively fighting for equal rights were understandably rankled.

On October 2, 1897, several local suffragettes, self-identified as "The Girls of Stockton," wrote to the *Evening Mail* to complain that Babe Bean was allowed to wear men's clothing, but they were not. "What puzzles us girls," they wrote, "is why Babe Bean should be allowed to dress that way, while if any of the rest of us wanted to walk out in that kind of costume for a change we would be arrested quicker than quick." They continued, "the *Mail*, which always has a sarcastic word for women. . . pats her and pets her while the police look on and smile." In conclusion, they said that they were all going to dress in men's clothing, go out to the houseboat, grab Babe and dunk her in the lake. Babe's response: "It is your privilege to dress as you see fit, whether it is after the fashion of Venus or after the fashion of Babe Bean. I wish to state that boys' clothes are still selling in Stockton at reduced prices. You are quite welcome to that information." Letters to the editor poured in to defend Babe's position with almost no support for "The Girls of Stockton."

About Stockton, Babe later wrote, "I should like to say a word for Stockton men. If the courtesy shown to me by the police department and the newspapers alike is a proof of what sons of this pleasant little burg are, then you have more good and generous fellows together here than it has been my lot to meet in any other one place."

No doubt this was a satisfying time for Babe, as she was adopted by the city of Stockton as she was and had no need for pretense. She had friends, a good job, a comfortable home that she loved, and a community where she could participate in public life in a relaxed and open manner. The *Stockton Mail* was so proud of her that the editors ran stories about her almost as much as they printed her articles. Numerous line drawings appeared of her at home in her "ark" and on the job chasing down stories, including one amusing cartoon of her hurrying after Governor James Herbert Budd along the street (she got the interview). The one and only known photograph of her was taken by a photojournalist named Ed McCullagh in October 1897 and appears at the beginning of this chapter.

Babe pursuing Governor Budd
(*Stockton Evening Mail*, **1897**)

By May of 1898 Babe had apparently tired of being mute. She was riding in her buggy two miles outside Sonora when a runaway wagon team crashed into her, causing her to be thrown from her buggy to the road. The accident, she exclaimed in a letter to a Stockton friend, completely restored her power of speech and she was overjoyed.

Though Babe had carved out a comfortable life for herself in Stockton, her sense of adventure was not yet satisfied. When Americans shipped out to participate in the Philippine Insurrection in 1899 she saw a chance to be a war correspondent. But women were not permitted in war zones or on naval ships. So thirty year old Babe did what she had to do to follow the action; she changed her identity and masqueraded as a man. As Beebe Beam, she got aboard the troop transport *City of Para*. When civilian passengers were rounded up for vaccinations, she was discovered to be a woman and the captain put her ashore in Hawaii. She took another ship back to California from there. However, she tried again, being more crafty, and she successfully made her way to the Philippines on her next attempt.

While there, Beebe Beam served as a Spanish language interpreter and nurse, living in military camps with the Sixteenth, Twenty-Ninth, Forty-Second, and Forty-Fifth United States Volunteer Infantry regiments. She did not participate in combat, but witnessed the Battle of San Mateo and joined several marches throughout Luzon. She accompanied United States military forces to Santa Cruz, Laguna de Bey, Camarines, Caloccan, and Manila. While on this adventure, Beebe got a tattoo of the American flag. She also wrote of her experiences, sending the articles home under two different pen names, one a man's, one a woman's, depending on the story.

Beebe never enlisted in the military, but after a year with the troops, she returned home and published "My Life as a Soldier," in the *San Francisco Sunday Examiner* magazine. Though her exploits abroad had been as a man, the story was marketed as that of a woman's experiences to showcase it as a novelty.

Upon her return, Elvira/Babe/Beebe moved in with her mother and sister Victoria in San Francisco, where she remained for a short time.

In 1903 San Francisco passed a law making it illegal to wear opposite sex clothing, which may have been the catalyst for Elvira's next reinvention. She would no longer be a woman who dressed like a man, but simply a man named Jack Bee Garland, "Garland" being Jack's mother's maiden name. Jack devoted much of his life to charitable work, particularly for the Red Cross. After the 1906 earthquake, he worked as a medic, and then became an unofficial social worker to the homeless men of the city. As an explanation of his interest in this type of work, Jack would tell of a heartless scene he witnessed in a charity's office in 1896 that convinced him to devote his life to helping the needy. That was the year his brother William died, but it's unknown if there was a connection. A slight, frail looking Jack could frequently be seen tending to the homeless on the streets of San Francisco wearing a faded blue suit, shoes purposely too large for his small feet, and a wide hat pulled low over his eyes. The fact that he often went out after dark might also have been part of his disguise. He eked out a living for himself by freelancing for local newspapers.

In 1912 Jack's mother Eliza died at the age of 77. The newspaper death notice listed three surviving children, the two married sisters and "E. V. Mugarrieta" with no indication of gender.

During Jack's later years, his sister Victoria Shadburne, who lived in Los Angeles, provided for his financial support. She had always feared that Jack's secret would lead to some violent end, but they remained emotionally close throughout their lives. Victoria referred to Jack as her "chum," and explained her sister's transformation as follows: "...suppose you had noble ideals and wanted to do things for your country. Suppose you were a woman, and the fact that you wore skirts instead of trousers prevented you from this. What would you do? Elvira did the only thing she could. She put on pants."[29] This is as far as Victoria could go in understanding her sibling. It was an explanation that satisfied her.

When Jack became ill with stomach ulcers in 1936, he didn't seek medical attention. Avoiding doctors was a common theme among transgender people of the day. Instead he kept going about his business until he fell unconscious on the street at the age of sixty-six.

After his death on September 20, 1936, Jack's sister Victoria provided the coroner with his real name and family history, and a spate of newspaper articles appeared about the "trousered enigma." Jack was buried in the family plot in a cemetery in Colma, California, in a white satin dress, a final indignity courtesy of his sister, who had tried to be accepting but was ill equipped to understand that her sister Elvira had long ago ceased to be.

V. WOMEN OF ILL REPUTE

Among the first women who came to California during the 1849 Gold Rush were prostitutes. Most of the men who arrived to seek riches left their families at home. Living conditions in California in those early days were less than acceptable for wives and children, especially in the mining districts. But even in San Francisco, the gateway to the mines, conditions were rough, at least in the first few years. The first prostitutes were mostly from Latin America. They set up camp in a tent city at the foot of Telegraph Hill, a notorious den of iniquity known as Chiletown where whoring, drunkenness, drug use, gambling, brawling, and murder were unrelenting.

The next wave of immigrant women included a ship full of French prostitutes who found that instead of earning a few sous from a Parisian, they could easily charge $100 for their wares in San Francisco, as the men were charmed by their European bearing and exotic accents. So rich were the California opportunities for French women that a shortage of prostitutes occurred in 1850 Paris. As the New York *Herald* put it, "Such is the Pleiad of brilliant stars who have deserted Paris for the city of San Francisco. A host of fallen angels, who go to purify themselves in a bath of gold, and who will doubtless revolutionize the shores of the Sacramento [River]." So many French prostitutes came to San Francisco that it briefly earned the nickname, "The Paris of America."

Prospects for entertaining lonely miners were boundless, and several enterprising women made an impressive financial killing in the business. They were aided by the fact that early California did almost nothing to discourage prostitution. With no established society and a haphazard justice system, the usual voices against the sex trade were largely absent.

San Francisco has long had a reputation as an "anything goes" type of city. This reputation is reflected in nicknames like "Baghdad by the Bay," a term coined by columnist Herb

Caen in the 1950s. At that time, long before U.S. military operations in Iraq, Baghdad was an exotic and faraway place to Americans, a multi-cultural and highly diverse city where a visitor could find any flavor of entertainment he or she desired. San Francisco had the same reputation from its inception, largely due to the Gold Rush that brought an immediate international population through the Golden Gate. In the same vein, the city's red light district became known in the 1860s as the "Barbary Coast." It was named after the African Barbary Coast, notorious for the same kind of predatory dives that targeted sailors. It was a three-block stretch of Pacific Street, now Pacific Avenue, between Montgomery and Stockton Streets, and featured dance halls, saloons, and brothels. The district was characterized by crime, prostitution, violence, and gambling. Said the San Francisco *Herald* at the time: "The upper part of Pacific Street, after dark, is crowded by thieves, gamblers, low women, drunken sailors, and similar characters. Unsuspecting sailors and miners are entrapped by the dexterous thieves and swindlers that are always on the lookout, into these dens, where they are filled with liquor—drugged if necessary, until insensibility coming upon them, they fall an easy victim to their tempters."

Gambling and prostitution coexisted in the large casinos and saloons where women were hired to work the roulette wheel, dice tables, to serve drinks, and to entertain the gamblers in any way required. Women in these jobs could make a lot of money, even if they avoided sex. Gamblers often paid women to sit next to them at the tables, or tipped them generously for bringing a drink, and of course they were paid by the saloon owner as well. There were 537 registered saloons in San Francisco in 1850, and there was little else for the men in town to do but drink and gamble.

The first brothel was reputed to be that of Irene McCready who came to San Francisco in April 1849 with her lover James McCabe who operated a gambling hall out of a tent. McCready's business started in a simple wood framed shack, but by 1856 she was able to purchase a two-story brick building to house her girls and entertain clients.

V. WOMEN OF ILL REPUTE

As the city evolved, many successful prostitutes became madams and opened exclusive parlor houses, lushly furnished bordellos where the clientele were carefully screened. Women who ran these houses often got rich and became local celebrities. They were the best dressed women in town and occupied an upper tier of society, openly associating both intimately and socially with the most influential men in the city.

But there were other classes of prostitutes, those who were indentured servants or victims of the white slave trade who were forced into the business by their overlords. Young women, in most cases girls, were brought to California from around the world to populate brothels. Notably, many Chinese girls were kidnapped or sold by their families for this purpose. The Chinese tongs in San Francisco ran the Chinese prostitution business, and they kept strict control. Many of these women were literally prisoners behind locked doors and barred windows.

**Chinese prostitute locked in a brothel,
1800s San Francisco**

There was also an even lower class of sex workers called "crib girls." They occupied squalid stalls in alleyways to ply their trade, and were victims of many hazards, including rampant syphillis and opium addiction. Women of many races and nationalities occupied these alleys, which were dangerous places not normally patrolled by police unless they were compelled to enter due to a murder or some other serious crime. Most of these districts met their end in the great fire of 1906, after which the property was put to more lucrative uses. One of these alleys is today's charming Maiden Lane near Union Square.

In 1852 the population of California was 200,000. Of those, only 20,000 were female. With each passing decade, the ratio of women to men would increase, but the balance of the sexes would not be achieved in the state for another hundred years. By 1950 the number of women and men finally achieved equilibrium.

But the prostitution business saw the end of its heyday long before that. By the 1880s, with the numbers of respectable citizens and permanent residents increasing, the city cracked down on vice with a heavy hand, raiding the parlor houses on a regular basis and forcing most of the major madams to shut their doors.

The last of the celebrity madams was most likely Sally Stanford who ran a bordello on Nob Hill in the 1940s, long past the peak of the classy brothels of the nineteenth century. A colorful and rowdy character, she named herself after Stanford University and went from being a madam to running a Sausalito restaurant, and was eventually elected mayor of Sausalito. In 1978 Dyan Cannon played Stanford in a TV movie

Sally Stanford

about her life. It was based on her autobiography of the same name, *Lady of the House.*

After Stanford's death in 1982, the city of Sausalito honored her and her dog Leland with a drinking fountain at the ferry pier. It is inscribed with the phrase, "Have a drink on Sally." Sally Stanford may have been the last of San Francisco's luminary madams, but she belonged to a broad panoply of wanton women cheerfully embraced by the city as part of its flamboyant history. There are entire books devoted to these women, but here we have space for only a few of the most outrageous and, obviously, the most notorious.

AH TOY (1828 – 1928?)
"China Mary"

Ah Toy by William Arista, 1852

Ah Toy (sometimes Ah Tay) was an exotic beauty, tall and glamorous with laughing eyes, only twenty-one years old when she arrived in San Francisco on a ship from Canton, China. It was 1849, the year after gold was discovered in

V. WOMEN OF ILL REPUTE

California. People from the world over were flooding in, hot with gold fever and feeling lucky.

The small town of San Francisco was then a chaotic montage of hastily-erected wooden buildings, tents, and military quarters. Every day ships choked the waters near the port, bringing legions of fortune seekers. The Chinese assembled in the district that would eventually become Chinatown. At the time, it was a collection of unsanitary makeshift shelters, a rough place with few women.

Some say that Ah Toy set off for America with her husband, who died en route. It would have been unusual, but not impossible, for her to have come on her own. She arrived during a brief window when Chinese women could immigrate as free agents. Of her motive for coming to America, she said she came "to better her condition." For many years after the Gold Rush began, Chinese girls and young women were sold as sex slaves to populate the brothels of San Francisco, but Ah Toy's arrival reportedly predated the beginning of this tragic practice. In fact, she herself became a participant in it once she was established in business as a brothel owner.

Almost nothing is known of her life prior to her immigration, though often-repeated fictions can be found online. As can a few photos, but all of these are of other women. The only image of her with any credibility is the one at the beginning of this chapter. It was painted by a young artist named William Arista who availed himself of Ah Toy's services and was so taken with her that he painted her portrait and kept the painting with him until his death in 1926.

Ah Toy was only the second Chinese woman to come to San Francisco and was the city's first Chinese prostitute. She played up her one big advantage over the other ladies of the night, the exotic mystery of the Orient. She spread the rumor that Chinese women were different from white women, even anatomically, and had special skills that inflamed the desire and curiosity of Western men. Ah Toy took advantage of this curiosity by charging up to an ounce of gold to allow men merely to look at her body. Thus began the first San Francisco peep show.

In those first few years, Ah Toy had the corner on the Asian prostitute business. She had the best of both worlds, Chinese men who wanted the familiar and white men who wanted the unfamiliar. In 1850 there were only seven Chinese women in town. There were 4,018 Chinese men. Ah Toy and her colleagues must have been very busy indeed!

After only two years, she had the money to start her own business. She returned to China where she purchased six girls from their families for $40 each. She then paid $80 each for their ship's passage to San Francisco, and installed them in her brothel on Pike Street, in what became Chinatown's Waverly Place. The unfortunate young women had little hope of paying off the debt they owed their madam. When she sold one of these women to a Chinese gambler or businessman, she was normally able to charge between $1,000 and $1,500, a nice profit on her investment. Ah Toy made money, opened another house and made more money. She paraded the streets of San Francisco in the most elegant European fashions of the day, preferring Western style clothes to Chinese.

The reputation of Ah Toy and her girls spread far and wide. She became the best known madam in San Francisco. With a boyfriend, John A. Clark, in the Vigilante police, she found some protection from the authorities for a time. Generally, the many brothels in the city were allowed to operate without much trouble, but Ah Toy ended up in court often enough when circumstances brought attention to her establishments. She was usually charged with keeping a "disorderly house" and one time with beating one of her girls. Once she was arrested when her Clay Street neighbors complained of the unsavory traffic. The *Daily Alta California* newspaper delicately described her house as containing "a number of valuable Chinese curiosities which cause a crowd there continually."[30]

Though one reporter claimed Ah Toy had been hauled into court over fifty times, she wasn't the least bit nervous about seeking justice in the courts herself. Nor was she worried about disguising the nature of her business. For example, once she brought a case accusing some miners of paying her in worthless brass filings instead of gold. She also had a man arrested for stealing her diamond pin. On that occasion, she entered the courtroom "blooming with youth, beauty and rouge, and bedecked in a decidedly [daring] bonnet and orange-colored shawl."[31] While the court waited for a Chinese interpreter to be procured, Ah Toy launched into an indignant lecture on the corruption of the legal profession.

By 1852 Ah Toy had gone from living in a shack to owning a brick mansion. But the law and anti-Chinese sentiment were to be her undoing in the end. Police raids became more frequent as the town became more civilized, especially against Chinese businesses. Then, in 1854, a law was passed prohibiting African Americans, Chinese, and Native Americans from testifying in court, making it impossible for Ah Toy to fight any crime committed against her. Coupled with the anti-prostitution law of 1854, which mainly targeted the Chinese, staying in business became tougher and tougher. The near constant police raids on her establishments eventually drove Ah Toy out of business.

On November 15, 1855, the "celebrated Chinese courtesan," as she was described in the press, tried to destroy herself with an opium overdose. A doctor induced vomiting and she survived. Her reason for attempted suicide was that she had no money and didn't want to live in poverty. Her rise had been quick, but her fall had been even quicker.

She sold her property and her girls for $800 each and left for China where, apparently, she found no greater fortune. She returned to San Francisco a few years later and was back in business, briefly. But for a Chinese prostitute, the good times were over. After retiring from the prostitution business, Ah Toy disappeared from public view. Nothing more is known about her life, but on February 2, 1928, a short article appeared in the San Francisco *Chronicle* announcing the death of a 99-year-old woman who had lived in the South Bay for decades. Her name was Ah Toy, aka "China Mary."

> Not much is known about 'China Mary', except that she had been here as long as anybody can remember. It is believed she was one of the first Chinese to come to California. Mary was supposed to be rich and was

connected with a prominent family in China. But she sold clams for what there was in it. She was known to yachting parties and fisherfolk for many years and to all old-timers in San Jose.

The Oakland *Tribune* added that she had lived in the "local Oriental quarter until the death of her husband about 25 years ago," and that she had a brother-in-law in Alviso known as "Chinese Louis."

Even though Ah Toy was not by any means a unique name among the Chinese immigrants of those days, perhaps China Mary really was the famous Ah Toy of our story. Either way, she left an enduring legacy in San Francisco history, even though her notorious career lasted less than ten years.

BELLE CORA (1832 - 1862)
"Queen of the Barbary Coast"

(*San Francisco Chronicle*, Dec. 1, 1890)

The story of Belle Cora began like that of many young women who drifted into prostitution after being used and jilted by a man. Hordes of such women have lived out their lives in complete obscurity, but Belle Cora was not one of those. Her name will live on in the annals of history, indelibly linked to the days of lawlessness, vigilante justice, and the end of an era in California.

Arabella Ryan was born in Baltimore, Maryland, in 1832, the daughter of a minister, a striking girl with dark hair and hazel eyes. At the age of seventeen, pregnant with an older man's child and kicked out by her father, Belle ran away to New Orleans, at that time America's premier gambling center.

After her baby died shortly after birth, Belle found work in a brothel.

She rose rapidly through the ranks to become one of the most successful of New Orleans' many prostitutes. She soon attracted the attention of dapper man about town and professional gambler, Charles Cora, an Italian-American with a thick mustache and dark, flashing eyes. When news of gold in California swept across the country, the couple couldn't resist the lure of adventure. They took off on a steamship to San Francisco in 1849 when Belle was just eighteen.

Fortune-seekers poured in from around the world, creating a paradise for the devil-may-care Belle and Charlie. They traveled from mining camp to mining camp winning a fortune at cards. By the following year, they had made enough money to open a lavish and ambitious gaming house in Marysville, California, which they named the New World gambling parlor. Prospectors and travelers stopped in to gamble on the roulette wheel and at the card tables, to drink at the sumptuous bar and flirt with the beautiful women. The venture was successful, so the Coras opened another gambling house in Sonora, California. The money kept rolling in. On November 17, 1852, they opened their third house on Dupont and Washington Streets in San Francisco, in what is now Chinatown.

The luxurious Cora House was a high-class joint by any standards. It was opulent and refined, part gambling house and part brothel. The city's most distinguished citizens frequented the establishment and were treated like royalty. The Coras offered their guests the best food and finest champagne. They had the most beautiful women on their payroll, and Belle Cora, as she now called herself, though she and Charlie had never married, was soon the most successful madam in the city. Her second parlor house in San Francisco was a well-appointed brick building on Pike Street opposite the Chinese brothel of Ah Toy (see previous chapter). For Belle and her Charlie, life was sweet.

In the 1850s gambling and prostitution were part and parcel of life in cities filled with single men, many of whom came into town with gold in their pockets. Truth be told, most

V. WOMEN OF ILL REPUTE

of those who got rich during the Gold Rush didn't do so in the mines. The successes were the men and women who provided services to the miners—people who ran hotels, general stores, brothels, banks, and saloons. The Coras came into town at exactly the right time to make a killing. And in those early rip-roarin' days, few people cared much about the presence of gambling and whoring. There were, in fact, hundreds of brothels in town, and just as many saloons and gambling halls.

But cities grow and change. The mad rush to the gold fields died down after a few years and people from the East moved into town with wives and children. They brought their prejudices and values with them. They didn't like certain groups of people, like the Chinese, and there were suddenly a wave of new laws limiting the freedoms of Chinese and tightening immigration policies to keep them out. They also had no tolerance for vice and lawlessness. In 1854 laws were passed outlawing gambling and prostitution in San Francisco, signaling that these activities were no longer acceptable.

Where Belle Cora had once been in the top social echelon of San Francisco, the best dressed woman in the city, and a successful businesswoman known by everybody, she was now being looked down on by the new infusion of "respectable" women.

One of those was the wife of General William Richardson, a U.S. marshal. On November 15, 1855, the Coras showed up at the American Theater and took their seats in the first balcony as usual for a performance of *Nicodemus*. At the intermission, Marshal Richardson, encouraged by his wife, tried to get the Coras thrown out. There was an argument, during which Richardson insulted Belle, calling her out as a besmirched woman and opening a wound that would fester.

A few days later, the two men met at the Cosmopolitan Saloon, had a drink, and shared a few incendiary words. Richardson threatened to slap Cora's face, but was stopped by the other men in the room. They met again at the Blue Wing the next day and seemed to have made up, leaving the bar in good spirits, but their whisky-laced tempers soon flared again. Cora grabbed Richardson by the collar of his coat, pulled out his derringer and shot the marshal dead. He was immediately arrested.

San Franciscans were so excited by the incident that they had an impromptu meeting to discuss the inefficiency of the law and the possibility of reorganizing the Vigilance Committee that had disbanded a few years earlier, an excuse to avoid due process and simply lynch the murderer. During its brief existence, the Vigilance Committee of 1851 had hung four men and exiled many more. No doubt the vigilantes felt that their version of justice was much more efficient than following the actual law. The restlessness of the crowd caused the sheriff to post fifty men to guard the jail where Charlie was being held.

Many in the city blamed Belle for inciting the murder, considering her more of an outrage to the decency of the city than Charles Cora. The San Francisco *Argus* indignantly objected to the fact that "the harlot who instigated the murder of Richardson, with others of her kind, are allowed to visit the theaters and seat themselves side by side with the wives and daughters of our citizens."

Belle spared no expense in Cora's defense, hiring the eminent attorney Colonel Edward Dickinson Baker, who was widely criticized for taking the case. He famously compared Belle to Mary Magdalene during the trial. After forty-one hours of deliberation, the jury was unable to agree, two opting for acquittal, six for manslaughter, and four for murder one.

This drove popular newspaperman and rabble rouser James King of William (a name he had given himself) to write an editorial proclaiming that prostitutes, gamblers, and the like were in cahoots with politicians, the courts, and law enforcement and that the system was corrupt. He alleged that Belle had bribed the jurors.

While Cora waited in jail for a retrial, another murder took place in the city on May 14, 1856. City Supervisor James Casey shot James King of William over a negative editorial he had written. King died on May 20. This second violent crime that left a prominent citizen dead, coming on the heels so soon after the other, sparked a general cry of outrage from the

V. WOMEN OF ILL REPUTE

public, who felt that lawlessness was out of control and should be dealt with harshly.

Impelled by the public uproar, the second Vigilance Committee of San Francisco sprang into being, anxious to make an example of somebody. An army of citizens came banging at the door of the Broadway jailhouse, demanding that Cora and Casey be turned over. The sheriff refused, but backed down when a loaded cannon was aimed at his door.

The Vigilance Committee tried the men under their own brand of justice. They found them both guilty, concluding that Cora's act was a deplorable assassination in cold blood. Both men were sentenced to death. Belle came to the prison and was allowed to stay with Charlie until his execution. They were legally married by a priest one hour before his death. He was hanged May 22, 1856, from the second story of Fort Gunnybags at Sacramento and Battery Streets, the headquarters of the Vigilance Committee. A crowd of thousands gathered to watch. Area newspapers concluded that justice had been done.

Hanging of Casey and Cora at Fort Gunnybags

Not everyone was satisfied yet, however. A letter to the Vigilance Committee was published in the San Francisco *Bulletin*, May 26, signed "Many Women of San Francisco," requesting that the vigilantes go one step further and boot

Belle Cora out of town as an example to show that such women were not welcome in San Francisco. This request went unheeded.

There was a backlash against the vigilantes headed by Colonel Baker, Cora's defense lawyer. It was called the "Law and Order" movement. They attempted to quash the vigilantes, but found that public sentiment was not on their side.

While the Law and Order movement was attempting to gain traction, the vigilantes took a former California Supreme Court judge into custody and very nearly hanged him too. They most likely would have done so if his friends in high places had not brought ships into the harbor threatening to pelt Fort Gunnybags with cannon fire. That judge was David S. Terry, the attorney associated with another of our notorious women, Sarah Althea Hill (Chapter VI).

Belle, now 24 years old, after several weeks of mourning, resumed her business. But without her Charlie she was an unhappy woman and developed an addiction to chloroform. She was only 29 when she died of the habit on February 19, 1862. She was buried in a cemetery in Colma, but years later, her body was disinterred and reburied beside Charles Cora at Mission Dolores in San Francisco where they share a headstone. The Cora House, their opulent gambling parlor, was pulled down in 1890 to make way for a new building.

Belle and Charlie represented the spirit of the times during the first days of the Gold Rush. They were the king and queen of a landscape characterized by vice and disorderliness. Their kingdom stood for only a few years, until traditional social norms and the rigors of decency were extended to embrace and reform the City by the Bay. That reformation, however, did not happen overnight, and the Barbary Coast, as the red light district was known in the 1860s, continued to support a multitude of sins for some time to come.

JESSIE HAYMAN (1867 - 1923)
"Diamond Jessie"

225 Ellis Street, Jessie's first brothel as it is today

In a city with no shortage of prostitutes and brothels, "Diamond Jessie" was a stand out as the proprietor of one of the poshest parlor houses in town. She was a smart businesswoman and made a fortune peddling sex to the high end market in San Francisco.

A redheaded knockout with a taste for diamonds, Jessie started her career in the 1890s at the brothel of Nina Hayman at 225 Ellis Street, an address with a colorful history. In the 1870s, the house was first put into service by madam Dolly Adams (Chapter VII). It continued to be used in that capacity until it was destroyed in the 1906 earthquake. Jessie used the name Jessie Mellon while a working girl, but her actual name was Annie May Wyant, and she was born in 1867 in New Orleans.

By the late 1890s, Jessie had become the house favorite. The Grand Duke of the Imperial Russian Empire, on a visit to

San Francisco, met the gorgeous Jessie and fell for her. He asked her to return to Russia with him, but she politely refused. In 1898 Nina Hayman married a wealthy lumber dealer and Jessie took over the business. As she made money, she invested in more property, and eventually ran a chain of parlor houses.

Like many others in San Francisco, Jessie was badly affected by the 1906 earthquake, which destroyed her house on Ellis St., but she opened the doors of her other properties to help feed and house the dispossessed in the chaos that followed the disaster.

It gives us a good idea of how important Jessie was as a business owner when in 1906 District Attorney Langdon began a campaign aimed at cleaning out "disorderly houses" in residential districts. He targeted her property at the corner of Post and Divisidero for his first arrest. His intention was to take out the queen of the hill. She was found guilty, but was not put out of business.

Houses of ill repute were usually able to operate without too much trouble from the local police, but in 1908 the federal authorities began to crack down on the white slave business, and Jessie was taken by surprise when she was arrested by U.S. Marshals for harboring an alien woman for immoral purposes. The alien was Englishwoman Ethel Southwood, whom Jesse claimed to have hired as a singer and pianist. She was found guilty and sentenced to 30 days in the county jail and a $300 fine, a much milder sentence than the law allowed. When she got out of jail she coolly returned to her business.

When Jessie acquired the property at 130 Eddy Street in 1912, her crowning glory, she turned it into a showplace that she called "an oasis from cares and time." For the grand opening of this *maison de joie*, Jessie had invitations printed and sent out to the society men in town. The place had a first rate wine cellar and lavish décor. Each room had a theme, like the blue room, Turkish room and French room. Furniture was imported from around the world to match the themes. Jessie's own suite was decorated in red and gold. She hired the best girls and treated them well. For all this, Jessie charged exorbitant prices. Her customers were those to whom money

V. WOMEN OF ILL REPUTE

was no object. She got richer and invested in other boarding houses. Her place at 44 Mason Street, for example, was said to be the most magnificent brothel west of the Mississippi.

During her rapid rise to wealth and fame, Jessie's beau was Allan St. John Bowie, a blue-blooded businessman and bon vivant. Jessie habitually registered as Mrs. St. John Bowie whenever she travelled, but there is no record of a marriage.

Jessie continued raking in the dough until around 1917 when tolerance for prostitution drastically diminished and running such a business became increasingly difficult. She retired a wealthy woman, her worth estimated to be close to a million dollars, $100,000 of it in diamonds. Though she and St. John Bowie remained good friends, he began to distance himself from Jessie during this time and denied that they had ever been married. Jessie remained single from then on.

On March 31, 1923, in the fashionable Cecil Hotel on London's Strand, fifty-six year old Jessie Hayman dressed for dinner, carefully choosing the appropriate diamonds to wear, then sat in a chair and unexpectedly died of a heart attack. Traveling alone, she was on the last leg of a three month tour that had taken her to Asia, India, Palestine, and Europe.

At the time of her death, her estate was valued at $250,000, and included $58,000 worth of bonds, stock in Louisiana oil wells, and property in San Francisco consisting of two apartments, one apartment house and two houses. She left most of her estate to her family members. For her two elderly Persian cats, Teddy and Beppo, she left $1,000 each to whomever would take them in, expressing the hope that it would be one of her grandnieces. The cat sitter reported that both cats quit eating at about the same time Jessie died, and Beppo died three days after Jessie. Teddy, however, survived and was adopted by one of the nieces.

After hearing that the bulk of the estate was to go to the children and grandchildren of a deceased sister, Jessie's brother Charles contested the will, claiming that Jessie had not been of sound mind when she wrote it and that his sister's family had taken advantage of her during her state of heartbreak after her relationship with Allan St. John Bowie ended. Eventually, the nieces settled with Charles, giving him $19,000.

Diamond Jessie was one of the last of the celebrity madams of San Francisco, possessing all the style and pizzazz of a movie star. Jessie was often heard to say, "I only go first class," and it couldn't have been more true.

TESSIE WALL (1869 – 1932)
"Queen of San Francisco's Nightlife"

Tessie Wall

Tessie Wall, who earned the title "Queen of San Francisco's Night Life" wasn't your run of the mill madam. She was the most successful of the lot. Like Jessie Hayman, her name will live on forever in the annals of the City's history while many another madam has long been forgotten.

Teresa Susan Donahue was born in the Mission District of San Francisco in 1869 to working class Irish Catholic immigrants, John and Sarah Donahue. Tessie had blonde hair and blue eyes. She married handsome Edward Wall, a fireman, when she was only fifteen, and had son Joseph with him in 1886. The child lived only a few months and, shortly after that, Edward deserted Tessie. Many years later she gained an official divorce.

Once she was on her own, Tessie went to work as a housekeeper for wealthy banker Judah Boas. This sort of life apparently did not appeal to her, as she then became a dance hall girl and a hard drinker. One day the heavyweight champion of the world, John L. Sullivan, stopped into the saloon to have a few. Right away, he noticed the buxom blonde bombshell Tessie and invited her to sit at his table and drink with him. The two of them downed several bottles of champagne, after which Tessie was still going strong, but the bulky Boston boxer could take no more. Tessie became known as "the gal who licked John L. Sullivan."

Tessie had business sense and managed to gather together enough money by 1898, when she was still in her twenties, to buy a boarding house in the Tenderloin at 221 O'Farrell Street, out of which she ran her first house of ill repute. The 1906 earthquake destroyed this property, so she bought another at 337 O' Farrell and was back in business stronger than ever. She employed between ten and fifteen girls who were under twenty and blonde, who looked, in fact, like herself, except that by now she had gained quite a bit of weight, weighing in excess of 200 pounds. In the words of the inimitable Herb Caen, "…town observers agreed that from the rear, Tessie looked like the silhouette of a ferry-boat sailing majestically into the setting sun."[32]

She treated her clients like kings and her reputation began to grow, as did her bank balance, and she was always decked out in fabulous diamond jewels. She frequented auctions where she bought decorations for her brothel, like red-shaded lamps, nude statues, fine lace curtains, expensive paintings, and deep pile carpets. She also owned a townhouse on Powell Street that was her home, and she decorated this as lavishly as she did the boarding house. Tessie made a lot of money, but she also liked to spend it, so she never became rich.

V. WOMEN OF ILL REPUTE

In early 1907 Tessie's Larkin Street house became the target of a series of police raids under the jurisdiction of Captain Mooney. In March of that year, Chief of Police Jeremiah Dinan made an interesting change to the districts, moving Larkin Street into the jurisdiction of the Central Station under Captain Martin. It was the only street redistricted, Tessie's "resort" being the most notorious business on the block. In later court testimony, Captain Mooney claimed that the chief had interfered with his efforts to close down the brothel. He claimed he was told by Dinan, "Let the poor devil alone. She is trying to make a living down there in the burned district and her house is straight."[33] It pays to have friends in high places.

As she neared 40, Tessie fell in love with powerful Republican political leader Frank Daroux, whose nickname was the "boss of the Tenderloin." On their first date, he took her to a chi-chi French restaurant where, legend has it, she drank twenty-two bottles of champagne!

Tessie had aspirations of being respectable and joining society, but as a madam, that would have been impossible. She began to dream of marriage and a different kind of life. Her association with Daroux was also problematic for his political career, though he was no saint, being the owner of several gambling dens. Still, men were not held to account for their sins the way women were, so marrying a madam would be a liability for Daroux. After much cajoling from Tessie, he agreed to marry her…secretly. They went to Pennsylvania and married on September 1, 1909. Among other gifts, Daroux gave her a fabulous gold-plated Napoleon bed.

Tessie kept up her campaign to be acknowledged as Mrs. Daroux, and by 1912 had persuaded her husband to go public, but only if she promised to retire from her business. The two were remarried at St. Mary's Cathedral after finding it nearly impossible to find a minister who would marry them, as both were notorious in the city as unrepentant reprobates. The priest of St. Mary's only agreed to do it if the ceremony took place in the rectory and without any guests, only two witnesses. Tessie was disappointed, as she wanted the grandest wedding the town had ever seen, but the reception was another story. Now that was a party! Champagne flowed to the tune of 960 bottles. Still, only a handful of respectable society women attended, though many of their husbands did. Society was not yet ready to give Tessie the green light. In fact, when the couple went house hunting, they were turned down at several ritzy apartment buildings.

The marriage was rocky, no big surprise considering the two characters involved. Tessie was still a big drinker and she also liked to go to the horse races. Frank had his own vices. He took up with a woman named Mary Lind, which enraged Tessie and led to intense quarreling between them. She threatened to kill the other woman. After eight years of marriage Frank decided he'd had enough and informed his wife that he wanted a divorce. He moved into the posh St. Francis Hotel. Tessie tried unsuccessfully to persuade him to return. After one failed attempt by telephone in February, she grabbed a kitchen knife and began to slash at her wrists. She was stopped by a friend who was in the house.

The divorce trial took place in the spring of 1917, and proved a popular diversion for the public, as the Daroux dirty laundry was liberally aired. When Frank testified that Tessie had injured his standing in society because she ran a brothel, her lawyer pointed out that he had married her knowing what she did. "Yes, but I was crazy then," he replied. "Are you crazy now?" asked the lawyer. "No," he answered. "I've had my eyes opened good and plenty since then."[34]

There was a lot of testimony regarding heavy drinking, verbal and physical battles, gambling, who had paid for what during the marriage, and Tessie's relatives even testified against her. She was portrayed as violent and unstable. Regarding her drinking, she said she had reformed in 1916 and now hardly drank at all. However, in December of 1917 she was arrested on a charge of public intoxication at a downtown hotel. Frank Daroux got his divorce.

On December 18, as he left his hotel, Tessie accosted him and the two of them argued fiercely as they walked down Powell Street, then Ellis and into Anna Lane (now Cyril Magnin) where things got really heated when Frank insulted Tessie beyond her endurance. She pulled a small revolver from her handbag and shot him three times in the chest, then stood over him where he had fallen, sobbing and proclaiming, "I shot him 'cause I love him, damn him!" Frank survived. Tessie confessed to the police that she had bought the gun to shoot his girlfriend Mary Lind, but he had provoked her into using it on him instead.

Frank refused to testify against Tessie for attempted murder, so the case was dismissed. The following year she spotted Mary Lind in a downtown restaurant and promptly pulled out her gun and fired. She missed.

Tessie appealed the divorce and in 1921 the trial took place. Frank was again the victor. A few months later he married Mary Lind and they moved to the East Coast, far from Tessie's rage. She never saw him again, but she never got over him. Frank died in 1928.

During Prohibition, Tessie ran a speakeasy serving Canadian whiskey to her friends out of her apartment in the Mission District. This small apartment was overflowing with furniture and décor taken from her O' Farrell Street boarding house, complete with the Napoleon bed Frank had given her. She had paintings of him on display in her home and several busts of Napoleon as well because she thought Frank resembled Napoleon. When she needed money, Tessie pawned pieces of her large diamond collection and kept herself afloat.

Tessie had shrewdly always been friendly with the police, and they had rewarded her by turning a blind eye. For many years, one of her civic honors was to be the Queen of the Policemen's Ball, where she appeared each year in an expensive low-cut evening dress, dripping with diamonds, on the arm of the city's mayor, Sunny Jim Rolph. She would slap a thousand dollar bill on the bar and say, "Drinks are on me!" making her even more popular. She led the Grand March in the Civic Auditorium up until her death.

Tessie died on April 28, 1932, at the age of 62 after suffering for three weeks from an ulcerated tooth. She went to the dentist, had the tooth removed, went home, then died an hour later. Her primary beneficiary was police captain John J. O'Meara and his wife, who were bequeathed a three-flat building and diamond jewelry. O'Meara had been a cop on

Tessie's local beat back in the good old days. Her other possessions were auctioned off in June in front of a huge audience of curious gawkers. The gold bed fetched a mere $105, and the entire lot of antiques and imported *objets d'art* went for less than $2,000.

Today, the two best remembered tidbits about Tessie Wall are that she drank John L. Sullivan under the table and that she shot Frank Daroux in front of the Tivoli Theatre because she loved him, damn him!

VI. ADVENTURESSES

In the nineteenth century, the word "adventuress" was used to describe a type of woman who single-mindedly, and through whatever means necessary, set out to land a wealthy husband. In those times, you might imagine, there was no limit to the number of women dreaming and scheming toward that goal. After all, few opportunities for wealth, status, or even survival were available to most females beyond their ability or luck in finding a mate. The primary occupation of most girls (and their parents) around the globe was to marry well.

But to earn the label "adventuress," a woman had to go much further than hoping, smiling profusely, and learning to embroider samplers. As the term was used then, an adventuress was a scheming, lying sneak who misrepresented herself to trap an unsuspecting man. She was a dangerous creature who landed a rich husband by trickery. She would, in the words of Lady MacBeth, "look like the innocent flower, but be the serpent under it." Her goal was always money, never love.

The term "adventuress" fell out of style by the early twentieth century when these women were called "gold-diggers," a label first popularized by the 1919 Avery Hopwood play *The Gold Diggers*. The best known gold digger of the early 20th century was actress and Ziegfeld girl Peggy Hopkins Joyce. Joyce married and divorced four millionaires and had numerous affairs with wealthy and successful men, amassing tremendous prosperity in the form of alimony, cash settlements, jewels, and property. She reportedly went on a million dollar shopping spree during a single week after her marriage to lumberman J. Stanley Joyce. Some have argued that she was the real-life inspiration for Lorelei Lee, the protagonist in Anita Loos' 1925 gold digger novel *Gentlemen Prefer Blondes*. Gold diggers were a common stock character in movies throughout the 1930s. In 1953 Marilyn Monroe starred in two films about gold diggers, *Gentlemen Prefer Blondes* and *How to Marry a Millionaire.*

Peggy Hopkins Joyce (Library of Congress)

Gold diggers were most easily identified when there was a significant age discrepancy between the woman and her husband, usually with the husband being extremely old. A modern example is model and *Playboy* playmate Anna Nicole Smith, who married 89-year-old billionaire J. Howard Marshall II in 1994 when she was 27, leading many to label her a gold digger.

VI. ADVENTURESSES

Today, both "adventuress" and "gold digger" have dropped out of common usage, as women, at least in most developed countries, can now follow their own professional ambitions and are not dependent on men for survival. There are still women who scheme to marry wealthy and powerful men, of course, but with so many other opportunities for personal development now available, there's not so much pressure to marry, and many women prefer financial independence, even if they are married.

The three women in this chapter doggedly went after rich men. And although all three of them were described as adventuresses for doing so, they fall into quite different categories. One of them was unequivocally an adventuress, setting out with a well formed plan to capture a rich husband. Another of them may have inadvertently drifted into such a plan of deception after more conventional methods of catching a mate had failed. And one wasn't actually an adventuress at all given the definition of the term at the time, but she was slandered as one. Still, she was no paragon of virtue, being a former prostitute and a parlor house madam. She was, interestingly, the only one of the three who succeeded in bagging her man. All three of these women were complex, fascinating and, need we even say it, notorious in their time.

SARAH ALTHEA HILL (1850 – 1937)
"The Rose of Sharon"

Sarah Althea Hill (Bancroft Library)

VI. ADVENTURESSES

Sarah Althea Hill, or Allie, as she was called by friends and family, had a look of vulnerability about her that caused men to lose their minds. She was beautiful and smart, but she was also calculating, tempestuous, and quick to draw a gun.

In 1871, twenty-one-year-old Allie and her brother Hiram Morgan Hill traveled from Cape Girardeau, Missouri, to San Francisco to seek their fortunes. They each had $20,000 received in trust from their deceased parents. It was a considerable fortune and certainly enough to last a long time if wisely invested.

By this time, after a brief two decades of existence, San Francisco had ballooned to a population of 200,000, a citizenry that included a good number of men (and some women) who had made the big time, either in gold, silver, railroads, or property. Those who were rich displayed their wealth ostentatiously, and San Francisco had rapidly become the capital of fashion, wealth, and prestige for the western half of the country. What better place for an aspiring young socialite, well educated in music and art, saturated with Southern charm, and at the peak of her beauty and marriageability? The world, or at least California, lay at her feet.

Allie's life was spent attending parties, drinking champagne in fine restaurants, going to the theater and the opera, and going for drives in the country with well-heeled young men in horse-drawn carriages. She went to such now historic places as the Cliff House for dinner and the Union Hotel for tea. Her "work" was to keep up an active social life, and that required the gravest attention to hair styles, dresses, shoes, hats and gloves.

During her first year in town, she was already popular and attracting attention. At an important New Year's Eve ball attended by the city's elite, including her brother, Allie got special mention in the gossip column of the San Francisco *Chronicle*: "Miss Allie Hill enchanted her numerous admirers in a robe of rich fawn-colored silk, with train and *panier*, the whole elaborately trimmed with cherry-colored velvet."[35]

Allie's brother, displaying the same level of breeding as his sister, hit the jackpot when he captured the attention of

Diana Helen Murphy, daughter of cattle tycoon Daniel Murphy. He married her, gaining a huge tract of ranch land south of San Francisco, land that would be named after him, eventually becoming the town of Morgan Hill.

Meanwhile Allie wasn't faring so well in the romance department. Although she was beautiful and cultured, her temperament kept getting in her way. She dated a prominent lawyer, Reuben Lloyd, on and off for several years, threatening often to kill him or herself (or his mother with whom he lived) if he didn't marry her. On one occasion, she went so far as to overdose on laudanum. Lloyd resisted, concerned about Allie's fiery and erratic behavior. She was not the demure Southern belle that she had appeared at the start of their courtship.

Even after Allie became pregnant, Lloyd refused to marry her. He arranged instead for her temporary removal to the country house of a wealthy black woman, Mary Ellen "Mammy" Pleasant. Mammy Pleasant was well known in the upper classes for her ability to make such problems quietly disappear. Allie's association with Pleasant, a famous figure in San Francisco history, would turn out to be a fateful happenstance for them both. When the child was born, Pleasant placed her in her own home, arranging her adoption by her housemates Thomas and Teresa Bell, who named the child Robina.

Allie's money was managed by her brother, who oversaw her investments, most of which turned out badly. Nine years after her arrival in San Francisco, Allie was nearly broke, still unmarried and feeling desperate. One day she showed up without an appointment in the office of William Sharon, the president of the Bank of California, ostensibly to ask his advice about investing. He had no idea who she was. She, like everybody in town, knew exactly who he was.

Senator William Sharon was one of the richest men in California. He owned the Bank of California and the magnificent Palace Hotel, as well as several smaller properties and a vast country estate at Belmont, south of San Francisco. He was sixty years old, a widower, and at the height of his wealth and power. If Allie had been aiming for the richest

VI. ADVENTURESSES

unmarried man in San Francisco, Sharon would have had a bull's-eye on his heart.

After a second meeting between them, the old banker took the bait. Before long, he had installed his latest mistress in a beautiful suite in the Grand Hotel (which he owned), across the street from the Palace Hotel, conveniently connected by a second-story breezeway. He paid her a handsome monthly allowance to come lightly tripping to his rooms whenever he wanted company.

This arrangement was agreeable for a while, almost a year, until Allie began to feel that her darling "Sen" was losing some of his original ardor for her. She had expected that after a few months of canoodling he would ask her to marry him, though, judging by his philandering history, there was no reason for her to expect this. Meanwhile, she had told everyone in the city that they were engaged. No wonder she was getting worried. She began spying on the senator, sneaking into his rooms to search his papers, accusing him of being with other women and generally making herself unpleasant. His response was to take away her key and forbid her from coming into his rooms unless he invited her. That made her angrier than ever, so she went to ever greater lengths to protect her investment. Once she even wriggled through the transom over the door and dropped down inside the room to look for clues to his dalliances.

She then turned to practitioners of magic for help, purchasing charms and spells to make him fall in love with her again. But he merely became more and more annoyed with her until he had finally had enough and told the manager of the Grand Hotel to evict her. He made her a generous cash settlement over a period of three years so she would have something to live on, but he ordered her to stay away from him. In fact, he instructed the staff that she was no longer welcome in the Palace Hotel. At least once, she was escorted off the premises when she tried to bribe an employee to let her into Senator Sharon's room.

Allie was terribly wounded by all this, as she had spent two years either with Sharon or trying to get back with him, and her reputation was ruined. Everyone knew she had been his mistress, so Allie was no longer welcome in society circles. She had even alienated herself from her brother Morgan, who was ashamed of her. She had an aunt, uncle and grandmother in San Francisco as well, all of whom turned their backs on her.

Mary Ellen Pleasant (Bancroft Library)

But Allie still had one friend, Mary Ellen Pleasant, who came to her aid with a new approach. It was clear that no amount of pleading or witchcraft was going to change Senator Sharon's mind about marrying her, but Allie believed that she deserved more than she had gotten, that this man had used her and tossed her aside and should have to pay dearly for that.

With Pleasant's advice and financial backing, Allie sued Senator Sharon for divorce, claiming that he had secretly married her in 1880, then he had abandoned her and committed adultery numerous times. She then produced a marriage contract as evidence, an informal agreement containing both their signatures and dated August 25, 1880.

The press went wild with this story, dubbing Allie the "Rose of Sharon." William Sharon flatly denied the whole thing, saying the woman had simply been his mistress. There had been no marriage, he claimed, no promise of marriage, and the marriage contract was a forgery.

So began one of the most lengthy, expensive and notorious legal cases ever fought in California. There have even been law books written about it. Among the attorneys on Allie's side were George W. Tyler and his son William Tyler. Later, they added skilled divorce lawyer, sixty-one-year-old Judge David Terry. Terry was a notorious character in his own right, whose younger days were full of colorful deeds from California's earliest (and rowdiest) days. Terry's greatest career achievement was his stint as a judge on the California Supreme Court in 1855 and his subsequent post of Chief Justice of the court the following year. He gained a reputation as an honest judge in a time when corruption at all levels of the legal profession was widespread and true justice was rare in the West. But his most infamous claim to fame was the killing of Senator David Broderick in a duel in 1859, an act that earned him the nickname "Terry the Terrible."

During the course of the trial, Judge Terry fell in love with Allie. Conveniently for the two of them, his wife died as the trial raged on.

There were suits, counter-suits, appeals and offshoot suits. There was a melodramatic interlude in which Allie went to jail for twenty-four hours for contempt of court. In court, as in life, she was irrepressible, volatile and happy to be in the spotlight. Each day several California newspapers put the story on page one, describing the high points of the day's testimony and giving a full account of Allie's demeanor, behavior and ravishing apparel.

The main witness called to prove the marriage was Allie herself. On March 11, 1884, she came to the stand for the first time. In anticipation of that, a huge crowd flooded into the courtroom to watch. She came up, according to the *San Francisco Chronicle*, "looking as demure, innocent and sweet as the arts of the toilet could make her." The article gave a full and detailed description of the plaintiff, noting her full lips, Roman nose, quick, gray-blue eyes, nervous expression, and luxurious auburn hair with its curls and ringlets under a bonnet decorated with butterflies.

Allie was a difficult witness to trip up. She could think on her feet. When it looked like she was headed for a trap, she was able to nimbly talk her way out of it. Lying had always been one of her greatest talents. It came to her as easily as breathing. Almost beyond himself with wonder, Sharon's attorney General Barnes observed, "She utters falsehood after falsehood, and finally, when brought to bay, says, 'Well, now I will tell you the truth'...and then she proceeds to utter a fresh batch of falsehoods with an adroitness that might well be envied by the father of lies himself."[36]

The trial went on for a year. The public was fascinated with Sarah Althea Hill. Some felt she was a naïve young woman who had been taken advantage of by a scheming, lecherous old man. Others felt that she was the devil. Either way, she was a celebrity, and she loved it. She wore a new dress each day to court and didn't seem to mind too much when she was characterized by witnesses as a forger, blackmailer and whore.

On the damp, misty morning of December 24, 1884, Judge Jeremiah F. Sullivan gave his decision in the case of Sharon vs. Sharon. Despite his recognition of a profound level of perjury, mainly by Allie and her friends, he found for the plaintiff, ruling that she was William Sharon's legal wife and would be granted a divorce on the grounds of willful desertion. He believed that the marriage contract had been signed by both parties, whatever Sharon's motives had been. Sullivan was influenced by the fact that the senator had invited

Allie's family members to his Belmont estate, had invited Allie to his daughter's wedding reception, introduced her to his son, and had gone with her to be introduced to her grandmother and aunt and uncle in their home. He would not have behaved that way, the judge reasoned, if she had been merely his paid mistress, as his treatment of his other mistresses demonstrated. Sullivan focused especially on Flora Sharon's wedding, saying, "I cannot believe that this man, this father, so far forgot his duty to the memory of his deceased wife, his duty to his daughter, his duty to the friends and guests who had assembled to do honor to the occasion, as to subject them to the polluting presence of a creature who differed from the common courtesan only to the extent that her commerce was with one man. He must in his heart have regarded her as more than a mistress."[37] She was awarded a handsome alimony and half of the community property he had acquired during their marriage, which was a tremendous fortune from any point of view.

Serves him right, was the general opinion, though many of this mind believed the marriage scheme was purely Allie's invention.

"I am so happy," she enthused the following day to *The Morning Call*. "I feel just like a young kitten that has been brought into the house and set before the fire....The poor, dear old Sen. I'm sorry I beat the old man, for I love him still; he's a dear, sweet fellow."

Allie immediately went on a shopping spree, buying Christmas gifts for her friends and servants, charging everything to "Mrs. William Sharon."

Meanwhile, her bitter ex vowed that she would never get a penny of his money and he immediately appealed. Allie lost the second trial. After that, David Terry, now Allie's principle attorney, pushed the case all the way to the California Supreme Court.

It was Mary Ellen Pleasant who bankrolled Allie's defense, paying her lawyers and buying her stylish wardrobe and jewelry. Pleasant was a rich woman, but the trials took a huge toll on her bank account and her reputation. She became widely known to the public through these sensational trials, and the details of her life that came out were severely damaging to a woman who had always tried to operate behind the scenes.

William Sharon also used up a huge amount of his energy and fortune on these cases, and he died before it was all settled. His son Fred and his lawyers carried on.

In 1886 David Terry married Sarah Althea Hill, much to the alarm of his children and friends, and brought her to live in his home in Stockton, California. But they did not settle into tranquil married life. Instead, they vigorously pursued their claim on Senator Sharon's estate. It was the thing that had brought them together, the thing they had in common, and inspired in both of them a deep sense of injustice.

The case finally came up in the state Supreme Court in August 1887 and was concluded at the end of January 1888. Allie was again victorious. The court upheld Judge Sullivan's original decision granting her a divorce. The Sullivan judgment was for $2500 a month alimony. The Supreme Court reduced the amount of alimony to $500 a month, the amount Sharon had been giving Allie all along.

But if Judge and Mrs. Terry were indefatigable in fighting this case, so were Senator Sharon's heirs. Fred Sharon revived an earlier court order that Allie must surrender the marriage contract, which had been declared to be a forgery in yet another trial. That crumpled piece of paper was her most prized possession. She refused to give it up and ranted wildly in court that the judge and other officials had been bribed to try to take it from her.

In 1888 Allie waved a gun around in the courtroom, threatening murder. Judge Stephen Fields ordered her removed from the courtroom, but when the marshal attempted to take hold of her, Judge Terry flew into a rage and punched the marshal in the face. After Judge Fields sentenced him to jail for six months, Terry vowed revenge and began making threats against Fields from his jail cell.

The following summer, Judge Fields came to California for his circuit duties with a bodyguard, Marshal Nagle. On August 14, 1889, they traveled by train from Los Angeles to San Francisco, stopping in Fresno, where, coincidentally, the

Terrys boarded the same train. When the train reached Lathrop station, both parties went to the dining hall for breakfast. Judge Terry saw Fields seated at a table with his bodyguard. He walked up to the judge and, without a word, slapped his face. Marshal Nagle stood, pulled his gun and shot. David Terry died on the spot, Allie kneeling at his side.

Nagle was arrested and tried. He claimed he had seen Terry reaching for a weapon, but Judge Terry's body contained no weapon. Nevertheless, Nagle was found not guilty and released.

Sarah Althea Hill, 1889 (Bancroft Library)

Allie then began a slow decline into insanity. She consulted spiritualists to try to talk to her dead husband. She walked the streets wearing dirty clothes and talking to voices in her head. She built a machine with wires that she talked into, claiming she was speaking to Judge Terry through it. She became paranoid and irrational, sometimes violent. She wandered the streets of San Francisco looking for her friend Porter Ashe, with whom she claimed she was in love.

Ashe's father had long been a friend and colleague to David Terry, and Ashe had been one of the few people who had remained friends with Terry and his wife after their marriage. The other friend who had remained ever loyal to Allie was Mary Ellen Pleasant. Between them, Ashe and Pleasant did what they could to help Allie with her living expenses, as she was by now practically penniless. She had never gotten a cent of William Sharon's money, and after her husband died, various creditors came to collect from his estate. Ashe's appeals to her brother Morgan for help met with "churlish replies."

By 1892 Allie's mental condition had deteriorated to an unmanageable state. She sat for hours in the bath talking to herself and pouring cold water over her head. She paced the floor all night, never sleeping. Doctors were called, but were unable to do much. For a time Allie stayed with Pleasant at the Bell mansion, but even her trusted friend could not heal her tormented mind.

Finally, Pleasant and Ashe reluctantly arranged for an insanity hearing. The presiding judge was Walter Levy, one of Allie's lawyers from her original team in Sharon vs. Sharon. Spectators packed in by the hundreds to witness the last chapter of the story that had occupied their imaginations for over eight years.

Allie told the judge that several people had tried to hypnotize her. She said she was full of wires and could transport herself via electricity to another world to get answers to her questions. Her discourse was rambling and sometimes incoherent. Several times she broke into laughter described as "hysterical" and "chilling." Mary Ellen Pleasant at one point was seen to be openly weeping.

VI. ADVENTURESSES

Allie was declared insane and Porter Ashe was appointed her guardian. She was sentenced to the asylum in Stockton, coincidentally the same hospital her husband had helped build.

When the time came and she realized she was being driven to the docks to take a ferry across the Bay, Allie became frantic and began fighting her attendants and yelling at the crowd of onlookers to save her from being locked up. More than a few men turned away with tears in their eyes.

Allie fought tooth and nail, literally, kicking, biting and scratching her attendants every mile of the ride from Oakland to Stockton, even at the doorway to the institution, struggling for her life not to be incarcerated. To no avail.

She was evaluated and diagnosed with "acute mania." Today she would most likely be labeled a schizophrenic. On the commitment register, her age was listed as thirty-five. In two weeks, however, she would actually be forty-two. The elegant four-story building surrounded by sprawling grounds and a high fence was to be Allie's home for the next forty-five years.

In the several years after her commitment, she was violent and disruptive. She was often restrained, and for several years, reports leaked out of injuries she inflicted on the staff and other inmates. As late as 1903 she attempted an escape, giving an attendant a black eye in the process. She also tried to get help from passersby through the fence and threw notes over it, claiming that she had been falsely imprisoned by her enemies.

The only visitors she had were writers doing research for articles and books. No family, no friends, not even her guardian, came to see how she fared.

In time, memories of the Sharon scandal and Judge Terry's murder diminished. People forgot about Sarah Althea Hill, and most of the characters in her story passed on. Allie gradually mellowed into a calm, dignified old woman with a regal bearing.

A nurse at the asylum who had been there 25 years in the early 1930s told a visiting researcher that Mrs. Terry had always been a most agreeable patient, but that she had heard of the difficulties the staff had dealt with in the early days. That visiting researcher was Stella Ingram Brown of San

Francisco, working on a book about Mary Ellen Pleasant. Brown likely visited the asylum around 1930, give or take a few years, when Allie was about 80. She described her as a short old woman with fine, bobbed, snow-white hair. Allie was heavy, weighing between 160 and 180 pounds. She wore a sapphire blue silk dress. Her eyes were still intensely blue and she was easily amused. She seemed to like the attention of her visitor, but evaded some of her questions, "particularly about her age."[38]

Another journalist, Evelyn Wells, came to interview Allie in 1936 and reported that the withered face retained the "perfume of desirability" from her youth. Allie remembered some things clearly, but was also plagued by delusions, recalling, for instance, that she had been married to Abraham Lincoln and Ulysses S. Grant.[39]

What was almost certainly Allie's last visit from the outside world came in July 1936 when two authors visited. Carroll D. Hall and Oscar Lewis were researching a book about the Palace Hotel (*Bonanza Inn: America's First Luxury Hotel*). They shared some details from that visit in the book.

"The neat, white-haired little figure sat in a rocking-chair. Her shoulders were stooped and she leaned forward slightly, regarding her visitors with bright, shrewd eyes. She had been unwell, her heart was bad, and some years earlier she had broken her hip, so it was hard for her to get about. A crutch was leaning against her chair; she kept her hand on it while she talked.... Small talk fell nimbly from her tongue.... She spoke politely, like a dutiful hostess, but she was not much interested."[40]

Throughout the interview, Allie sounded surprisingly rational after forty-four years in an insane asylum and, in some ways, very much like her younger self, as when the subject of the Palace Hotel came up. "That's my hotel, you know," she said. "It was built for me."

When asked about Judge Terry, she said, "He was one of my husbands. He was a big man." About Senator Sharon, she said, "He was a rich man. He owned the Bank of California. Is he dead?"

VI. ADVENTURESSES

They asked her about Mary Ellen Pleasant. "She was a black lady....Took charge of my trial. She was *smart*.... Is she dead?"

Allie died of pneumonia following on influenza on Valentine's Day, 1937. Newspapers all over the country ran the news of her death with headlines like "Famous Belle of Early Days Dies in Obscurity," but most of the readers would never have heard of her. She outlived her fame. She had blazed like a comet through 1880s San Francisco, riveting the country. She was a woman who had craved attention and adoration, who had wanted to live in the spotlight. She did, briefly, and paid dearly for it.

The hospital staff knew of no relatives (her brother had long since died) and made plans to bury her in the hospital cemetery. Thankfully, that did not happen. The remains of thousands of patients buried there lie in unmarked graves today, as the cemetery has been neglected for decades. When Judge Terry's granddaughter, Cornelia Terry McClure, heard that Allie had died, she kindly offered her a burial in the Terry plot, an action her father Clinton would surely have protested if he had been living.

"I have had no contact with Mrs. Terry all these years,' Mrs. McClure said. The whole affair was so tragic to our family. But I cannot permit Mrs. Terry to go to a pauper's grave, so I will take charge if we do not find nearer relatives."[41]

Allie outlasted almost everybody who had known her, but most of her life was lived imprisoned in mind and body. Her world was tiny. Even in death, she traveled just a couple of blocks to her final resting place at the Stockton Rural Cemetery beside the man she had loved.

Her greatest ambition was to be fabulously rich. In that, she failed, except in her own mind. She held court in the insane asylum with the staff as her servants, imagining the buildings and grounds as her estate. She wrote "checks" for large sums, and entertained the nurses with tales of champagne suppers, theater nights, and high society parties in gay old San Francisco. In that way, she ultimately did achieve her goal and became a great lady.

MAUD NELSON (1865 – 1902)
"Mrs. Charles Fair"

Maud Nelson, 1894 (*San Francisco Call*)

Caroline "Carrie" Decker Smith was born in Liberty Corner, New Jersey, May 13, 1865. She was the youngest girl of seven children, with only her brother William born after her in 1868. Her father Jefferson was from Canada and worked as a tailor in the town of Bernards. When Carrie was two, the family moved to Newmarket, New Jersey, where Jefferson Smith worked as a wagon driver for a clothing factory. His wife also worked at the factory as a seamstress. Some of the daughters, when they were old enough, also got work at the clothing factory, and the family made ends meet. Perhaps overwhelmed by the size of his family, one day not long after their last child was born, Jefferson Smith went off to work and never came home.

Carrie was pretty, blonde and charming. According to her mother, she was "vain and flighty." Her older sister Elizabeth described her as different from the other children. "All of us were workers," she said. "I worked around the house and my other sisters worked in factories —all but Carrie. She did not like to work. She used to read a great deal, and had a way of making us do things for her."[42]

When she was a teenager, Carrie and her mother clashed so much that she went to live with her older sister Sarah in Newark. Sarah ran a boarding house and soon put Carrie to work waiting tables, where she entertained the male boarders by flirting with them. But Carrie wasn't happy having to wait on anybody, so at sixteen, naïve and starry-eyed, she ran away to New York City to pursue her dream of being an actress.

Her family didn't hear from her for five years, during which time her mother married Abraham Nelson, who died after producing one son with Hannah. When Carrie did finally turn up to visit her mother, she was transformed into a radiant, tall, sophisticated, well dressed woman who looked like a true success story. But she was evasive about what she'd been doing for the previous five years. It's no surprise that she didn't want to talk about it. She had not made her name on stage after all, but she had learned a trade that paid well for a beautiful young woman with a head for business and no marketable job skills.

Carrie was soon off again. She traveled from place to place, not staying anywhere very long and changing her name at each stop. "She wrote often to mother and us," said her sister Elizabeth. "We thought it strange that she traveled around so. Once we heard she was married in Chicago, and wrote to ask her. She wrote back telling us never to mention the subject again. And we never did."[43]

After Chicago, Carrie went to Denver, and eventually landed in San Francisco around 1888 where she went by the names Carrie Smith, Maud Thomas, and ultimately Maud Nelson. She worked as a high-class prostitute, calling herself a "tailoress," which was a common device in those days, though such women usually used the term "seamstress" in city directories and telephone books. Maud was smart, she didn't get into trouble, and had good business sense. Within two or three years, when she was still in her twenties, she had saved enough money to buy a boarding house at 404 Stockton Street, and entered into business as a brothel owner.

Maud made money with what the papers routinely called "a questionable resort" and arrayed herself in the latest fashions, jewelry, and hair styles. She was described as beautiful, buxom, and plump. It wasn't long before she sashayed her way into the heart of Charles Lewis Fair, the son of the wealthy silver baron, Senator James G. Fair, one of the most prominent citizens in California. Charlie was known to be a rakish, wild young man prone to gambling, running around with women, and drinking heavily, but he was still considered to be one of the most eligible men in the country, and many a young woman had tried to catch his eye. But he had been well warned by his father to avoid getting himself trapped into marriage by a fortune hunting female. So far, he'd had his share of fun and managed to keep one step ahead of them. But Maud was different, reasoned Charlie. Obviously, she wasn't after his money. She had her own business and plenty of money. In fact, she and Charlie had a good time on her money, as he had not yet come into his inheritance.

Maud described Charlie as "a hard case" and was bent on taming him. Where his father had failed to reform his son, Maud had some success. She was able to bend Charlie to her will. Soon they were inseparable. They went to the East Coast to race Charlie's horses, then they took a few months to travel through Europe. When the couple arrived back in New York, Maud invited her family to visit. She put up her mother and sisters in the stylish Hotel Netherland and gave them a time like none of them had ever seen before. Charlie and Maud then returned to the West Coast.

The scandal produced by the relationship of the indiscreet senator's son and the madam was nothing compared to what was coming.

Maud sold her boarding house in October 1893 and three days later, on October 13, much to the shock and horror of the

Fair family and dozens of fervently hopeful young women, she and Charlie were married. On their wedding day, they secretly took the ferry to Oakland, hired a hack to take them to the records office for a wedding license, then told the driver to take them to a minister, any man of the cloth who could marry them, and they ended up at St. John's Episcopal Church on Grove Street, where a couple of witnesses were rounded up and the deed was done. One newspaper headline read, "A Disgraceful Misalliance."

Charlie's father was outraged that his son had managed to get himself "caught" by a scheming adventuress. He threatened to disinherit the boy to show "that woman" that she might not have made such a lucky match after all. James Fair couldn't have objected to his son consorting with a fallen woman. He himself was a notorious philanderer whose wife had divorced him for his sexual liaisons with madams and prostitutes. They were okay to dally with, went the prevailing male sentiment, but they were not okay to marry.

But even without his father's fortune, Charlie was destined to be a multi-millionaire. His mother had left a million dollars in trust for each of her two sons, to be given to them when they turned thirty. Charlie's brother had died, so Charlie was to get two million in just four years.

It was clear that Senator Fair hadn't quite given up on his son when he stated a couple of days later that Charlie could easily get out of the marriage when he sobered up and came to his senses, that any judge would declare such an outrageous marriage non-binding. But Charlie was in an entirely different state of mind. He was happy. So was Maud. Despite the widely held opinion of kith and kin, the two had married for love, and Maud was not an adventuress, as she was frequently portrayed.

Charlie and Maud got on a train and traveled east. For Maud, who had always valued her privacy, she was now suddenly notorious. The couple was dogged by reporters who wanted to write about their every move, what they wore, what they ate, what they said. Maud was frequently asked if she had been the proprietor of a house of disrepute. She emphatically denied it and took affront at the mere suggestion.

The newlyweds then sailed for Europe. When they returned from their honeymoon, they bought an apartment on Van Ness Avenue and settled down to placid domestic life.

Soon after her marriage, Maud began sending money every month to her mother and her sister Laura. She then bought houses for her mother, brother William, and sister Elizabeth. She was the proverbial prostitute with a heart of gold. She routinely helped anyone and everyone she found in need. In fact, she read the newspapers to seek out misery she might be able to alleviate, so powerful was her need to do good. There were many people in the city who received monthly allowances from her, and her reputation as a generous philanthropist was well known throughout San Francisco. After a questionable beginning for Mr. and Mrs. Fair, they had become a power couple who contributed greatly to the welfare of their community.

In 1894 James G. Fair died. His will stipulated that his fortune be divided between his two daughters and his son. Predictably in cases where there is a fortune at stake, myriads of fortune hunters crawled out of the woodwork and claimed to be secret wives and illegitimate children entitled to a share of the treasure. With Maud's steadying influence, the family was reunited to fight the onslaught of bogus claims. She won the sisters over and they became friends. In February 1896 Charlie got access to his inheritance, fifteen million dollars. When he turned thirty, he also got the two million left to him by his mother.

The Charles Fairs remained in San Francisco, continued to do charitable work, and lived respectably at ease among the fashionable set.

In May 1902 Charlie and Maud traveled to France to visit his sister Virginia, who had married a Vanderbilt. Charlie was also keen to drive the superior French roads, for he had a passion for automobiles, and was renowned as a first-rate driver and mechanic. While there, he bought a Mercedes Special with a 45 horsepower engine capable of going 85 miles per hour. He proceeded to race it all over the country, driving so fast that onlookers said they couldn't tell the color of the vehicle.

On August 14 he and his wife, with their chauffeur as passenger, were returning to Paris from his sister's villa at Trouville, and as usual, Charlie drove as fast as he could trying to break his brother-in-law's record of two and a half hours. As they shot through the village of St. Aguilin and approached the Chateau Buisson du Mal, one of the tires blew. The chateau gatekeeper's wife was the only witness. She described how the car slid sideways from the right to the left side of the road for about sixty yards. It then dashed up an embankment, turned a complete somersault and crashed into a big elm tree in front of the chateau gate. The chauffeur was thrown out of the car and landed in a ditch. Bloodied but conscious, he staggered to his feet and called for help. The Fairs, however, were both fatally injured, crushed by the vehicle and so torn up as to be unrecognizable. Charlie was thirty-five. Maud was thirty-seven. Their mangled bodies were shipped back to San Francisco, autopsied, and sealed into the Fair Mausoleum in Laurel Hill.

Maud had always promised her family that they would be financially provided for as long as she was capable of providing for them, and her will did provide for all of them. She left her mother $2,500 a year for life. To each of her siblings, and the child of a sister who had died, she left $10,000. The remainder of her estate, which was valued at $300,000, she left to her husband. The terms of Charlie's will were similar, except that his wealth was considerably more, estimated to be around ten million. The Fair family became worried that Maud's relatives might seek to claim the Fair fortune as well because the provisions of both wills hinged on which one of the couple died first. If Charles died first, all of his estate would go to his wife, and thence to her family after her death. If she died first, the reverse would be true.

When Maud's mother arrived in San Francisco, the Fairs wined and dined her and treated her like an old friend. They then made a deal with her in which she was awarded the entirely of Maud's money, but relinquished everything else belonging to the couple. Hannah seemed happy with the agreement until everybody started telling her she'd been taken advantage of. It was then that Hannah decided she needed a lawyer of her own. The case ended up in court.

Attorneys clamored for the attention of "poor and humble" Hannah Nelson, eager to represent her. Chandler and Beekman were awarded the case, traveled to France, and conducted interviews with a dozen witnesses who gave depositions leading to the conclusion that Maud had survived her husband by at least half an hour. Two witnesses claimed to have been bicycling on the road where the accident occurred. They said they saw the crash and heard Maud moaning after they confirmed that Charles was dead. Their testimony, it turned out, was entirely made up, and they were charged with perjury. The physician who had initially examined the bodies in France originally concluded that both parties had died instantly, but "on later reflection" stated that he believed Mrs. Fair had survived her husband by several minutes. The autopsies performed in San Francisco were inconclusive about who died first, but extremely grisly details were introduced by the Fairs' attorneys to demonstrate how Maud most certainly died first when her head was dashed into a tree. Ultimately, neither side could irrefutably prove who had died first.

The case was not fully settled until May 1904. Between them Maud's mother and siblings split about two million, making them wealthier than they could have dreamed. If they had ever had any qualms about where Maud's money came from, they didn't let it bother them. Hannah Nelson was 70 years old when her daughter died. She herself died in 1905 a very rich woman, thanks to the "vain and flighty" daughter who chose to run away from home rather than wash dishes.

VI. ADVENTURESSES

VESTA HASTINGS (1866 – 1898)
"The Countess de Henriot"

Vesta Hastings at the Palace Hotel

Though Vesta Hastings lived in San Francisco less than a year, she created a sensation while there and was faithfully followed by the local press for the rest of her life. She is one of many nineteenth century characters whose adventures are inextricably tied to that stomping ground of the rich and famous, the Palace Hotel. It was, after all, the place to be if you were somebody, or if you wished to appear to be somebody.

It was November of 1892 when a mysterious and flamboyant twenty-six year old woman strolled into the Palace Hotel lobby with numerous designer trunks and two maids in her wake. She wore a long dark veil, was dressed entirely in black, and was drenched in diamonds and pearls. Each finger carried two to four rings, and the little finger of her left hand displayed an immense ring in the form of a snake, sprinkled with diamonds and a huge ruby eye. Everyone present turned to watch as the woman sashayed to the front desk and registered as Vesta Doré Hastings.

During the days that followed, the Palace denizen would learn that this young woman with hazel eyes, creamy skin, and lush auburn hair spoke several foreign languages fluently, that she smoked Turkish and Egyptian cigarettes and drank the best champagne, and that she was a countess, the Countess de Henriot, by virtue of having married a French count who had been killed in a duel. The countess received postcards, letters, and flowers regularly at the hotel, addressed primarily to the Countess and Viscountess de Henriot, though also to "Miss Vesta Hastings."

Needless to say, the young widow with good taste in food and drink and a seemingly bottomless pit of money, attracted a lot of attention. Well-to-do bachelors flocked to her rooms, and lavish parties ensued. The countess bought food and drink for her guests, and they showered her with gifts, primarily of the jewelry variety.

Vesta talked freely of herself to her attending admirers, who learned that she had been born in France to a French father and a Russian mother. At the age of six, her family moved to Charleston, S.C., where she was raised. Her mother had since died, she explained, but her father was still living in Charleston. She had traveled extensively in Europe where her beaus were legion. Even King Leopold II of Belgium, she said, had fallen at her feet. But she'd settled on the dashing young de Henriot. After he was killed fighting for her honor, she had decided to return to the United States, and here she was, much to the delight of a throng of deserving young men crowding her rooms.

By all accounts, the Countess de Henriot was not a great beauty, but she was vivacious, flirtatious, and fun, if not a little enigmatic, which is always helpful in attracting attention.

Among Vesta's suitors was a millionaire named John Bradbury who was soon leading the pack in her affections. He had met her in Los Angeles and followed her to San Francisco, leaving behind his fiancée, Jennie Winston. By the spring of 1893 Vesta put it about that she and "Mallory," as she called Bradbury, were engaged to be married.

Everything was going along swell for "the beautiful Russian," as she was known, until Harry Carpenter, another of

VI. ADVENTURESSES

Vesta's would-be lovers, became jealous of Bradbury and started talking to reporters.

He said he had known Vesta the previous year in New York where she had been, not a Countess, but an aspiring actress, and that he believed Vesta was trying to steal Bradbury's fortune by tricking him into marriage. Once Carpenter spilled the beans, other New York men about town who had been keeping their counsel admitting that they had been quietly amused at the unsuspecting San Franciscans falling all over the erstwhile actress.

San Francisco reporters consulted their New York sources and confirmed that Vesta Hastings had recently been a stage actress there. They also found that she was a figure of some renown in Manhattan due to her ostentatious jewels and wardrobe. She had often been observed promenading in the latest European fashions. Vesta was a fashion leader, in fact, being the first to wear silver link girdles and crinoline, for example. "If the mode required big hats," said the *Examiner*, "Vesta Hastings balanced on her shining locks the biggest hat seen on Upper Broadway, and if the mode demanded toques her little head was fitted into the smallest bit of headwear that could be called a covering."[44]

Vesta laughed the publicity off, calling Carpenter a "cocaine fiend." Yes, she admitted, she'd tried her hand at acting when she'd first come back to the States. She'd always been interested in the stage. "I'm wealthy enough to indulge in my whims," she said. But she stood by the particulars of her back story and insisted that she had no intentions of hurting Bradbury, that her engagement to him had been entered into in good faith. In fact, she said, she had paid for his meals, paid all her bills with her own money, gave him expensive gifts, spending at least as much on him as he had on her, all of which appeared to be true. But as to their engagement, when Bradbury heard the stories, he denied that he had ever had any intention of making her his wife. Perhaps the pan was getting a little too hot for Bradbury, since the folks back home, including Jennie Winston and family, were none too happy with his escapades in San Francisco. Also, more and more information was leaking out about Vesta's past, and despite her protestations, it appeared that the entire countess bit was an act. Well, she was an actress after all.

The press kept digging. Eventually, by April, the truth emerged. The Countess Vesta Doré Hastings de Henriot was actually Blondena "Bonnie" Riley, the daughter of widower R.R. Riley, owner of a lumber yard in Portland, Oregon. Both of Bonnie's parents were Irish, and her family was among the early settlers of Eugene, Oregon.

Her history was pieced together by talking to old friends and relatives back in Portland. Bonnie was bold, rebellious, and self-indulgent, even as a young child. After her mother died, she was sent to a convent, but was soon put out as incorrigible. When she was a teenager, she attended the exclusive St. Helens Hall in Portland; however, she was expelled from the school for improper liaisons with men. She was then sent to Harrisburg, PA, to study at Miss Woodward's Seminary, but was expelled from there as well. By this time she was sixteen and already had a habit of parading about in fine clothes and lavish jewels, though she had little money of her own. But she learned early on how to please men who had money.

When she returned to Pennsylvania with aspirations of being an actress, she had taken the stage name Vesta Dora Hastings. She began getting parts on the Philadelphia stage, where she appeared in 1889 and 1890. In 1891, she moved to New York and joined the well-known Nat Goodwin company. She appeared in minor roles in *The Case of Clemenceau* with Nat Goodwin, and in an operetta by Ermina R. Steiner entitled *Flourette*. Those who knew her said she was bright and intelligent, ready with a laugh, a fascinating "little elf."

Vesta soon hitched herself to a wealthy and well-connected dry goods merchant, who put her up in an expensive apartment on West Thirty-Fifth Street with multiple servants at her disposal. Her boyfriend let her have anything she fancied from his stores, and he paid for paintings, furniture, statues, and tapestries for her apartment.

After about a year of this royal living, during which Vesta's acting career floundered, her man went abroad. She followed, but he made it clear that their relationship was over.

When she returned to New York, she took up with the nephew of a prominent city official, and so was able to continue her opulent lifestyle for a time. But by the summer of 1892, when she was twenty-six, Vesta was running low on resources. She thought of her dear old father and returned to Portland for a visit, having been out of touch for several years. She told her family that she'd married a count and had two babies who were currently in Australia awaiting the return of their mother. She needed money to get back to them and persuaded her father, who was rapidly drinking himself to the grave, to part with $4,000, playing on his sympathies with the thought of those two nonexistent grandchildren.

Newly bankrolled and with a new identity, the Countess de Henriot headed for San Francisco, a city rolling in wealthy businessmen. For six months, she had pulled off an elaborate deception and very nearly caught herself a rich husband. But he slipped the net.

John Bradbury returned to Los Angeles in May 1893. Vesta went after him, proclaiming to one and all that she really was a countess and she really was in love with Mallory. But she had no luck wooing him back, and blamed his family for coming between them.

Back in San Francisco, Vesta continued her partying with the many other suitors. But the jig was up and despite the free champagne, the suitors began to recede from her side. She was now routinely maligned as "an adventuress" in the press.

As the Seattle *Post-intelligencer* put it, "The San Francisco businessmen don't mind losing their diamonds and their dollars, but to be duped by an Oregon girl, who isn't a countess but a Riley, is too much."[45]

The newspapers had a ton of fun with this story. The San Francisco *Examiner* asked the question, if she could pin any title she wanted on herself, why'd she go for countess? Why not duchess or princess? Very likely she thought it would be easier to pull off a lesser title.

Now completely outed as simple Bonnie Riley, Vesta packed up and left San Francisco.

In June she arrived in New York with a plan of going to Paris to put as much distance as possible between her heart and John Bradbury. However, in August she returned to Los Angeles, apparently still sweet on the young millionaire. He must have given her some reason to hang on because it came out later that he had made arrangements for her lodgings and her landlady knew him well. At every opportunity, Vesta, still going by the name Countess de Henriot, told reporters that she and Bradbury were soon to wed.

Nevertheless, in early December, Bradbury traveled to Oakland with Lucy Banning, a woman endorsed by his parents, where they were hastily married. Vesta immediately left Los Angeles, but she was sighted in California several times after Bradbury got married, either in L.A. or San Francisco. A *Chronicle* reporter happened upon her on a ferry boat and noted that she had changed. She wore no flashy jewelry and her hair had been dyed almost black. She denied her identity at first, but he pressed her and she finally admitted she was the one and same Countess de Henriot. When asked where she was going, she said she would stay in San Francisco another five days, then she was on her way East to take a ship the first week of February to Liverpool. "I shall visit London," she said, "and then go to Florence, Naples, Paris, and several other cities. Then I shall depart for Cairo. It has long been my desire to spend some time in Egypt."[46] When asked about John Bradbury, she said that was between the two of them, but she then proceeded to talk a blue streak about him. She said she still loved him, but strongly denied the rumor that she had gotten a $2,000 settlement from him to avoid a breach of contract lawsuit.

Vesta didn't go to Egypt. All the high living had drained her bank account. If she had invested all of the effort and cash into the countess plot to capture a wealthy husband, as many believed, she had failed.

But she was not to be counted out just yet. Vesta's father died at the end of 1893, leaving her and her brother a solid inheritance of $25,000. She took her cut and bought a mansion in Paris where she could live the kind of lifestyle to which she felt entitled. That lifestyle included a never-ending stream of admirers, suitors and lovers, but Vesta had given up the idea of marrying. Why should she, she said. She was having the time of her life. She created a sensation wherever she went, and was frequently sighted at Maxim's and the theater, a tiny fox terrier in her arms.

Vesta had trifled with many a lover's heart, but the day finally came when her own heart was broken. She had fallen in love with a man who had tired of her. At a large dinner party that both of them attended, he announced that he was going to marry another woman. Within the hour, a mortified and distraught Vesta threw herself from a second-story balcony. Though badly injured, she didn't immediately die. It took four days for death to free her of her pain. She died on October 30, 1898. She was thirty-two. A huge crowd showed up at her funeral, then she was buried in an unmarked grave, per her request.

In her will, Vesta left a good portion of her estate to her friend, M. Leblois, a butcher in the Rue de Courcelles. Presumably, she had so renounced Bonnie Riley that she had split completely with her brother and his family. Nobody she knew in France was aware of her real name. Estate agents published notices in the papers looking for heirs of Vesta Hastings.

Much of the press that followed her death highly romanticized her life, repeating some of her own stories as facts and making her out to be a fabulous beauty, a flawless gem of breeding and culture who attracted nothing but praise from all who knew her. But the facts suggest that the following description by the Washington *Evening Times* was closer to the truth.

"Vesta Hastings was neither pretty nor clever, nor did she possess any charm that was notable, but by pure effrontery and some mysterious fascination, she crowded into ten or twelve years more luxury and gaiety and so-called enjoyment than many noted women of her class could compass in a lifetime."[47]

VII. PERFORMERS

In a book about notorious women, you'd expect a category for performers, as the stage arts have traditionally given us so many eccentrics. Though California in its early years was not known as an artistic center, a few important actors, singers, and dancers were born or were based there.

In the early years, California was so isolated from the major population centers of the United States by geographical distance that there was nothing casual about traveling there. It could take two or three months just to get there, so it wasn't a popular venue for a traveling show. But some entertainers relocated to the West Coast, looking for new opportunities, like the family of Jeanne Bonnet (Chapter IV). Some of the miners too, once they hung up their gold pans, found a new vocation on stage.

During the Gold Rush, women came to the mining camps to entertain the sourdoughs, as the California miners were called. Most of these female entertainers were prostitutes, but miners craved other kinds of entertainment as well, and a few hardy singers and dancers traveled the camps to put on shows in wood plank dance halls. Anything more sophisticated than that took place in the cities of San Francisco, Sacramento, and Stockton.

One well-known entertainer didn't have to travel to the mines to perform. She was already there, as she had come as a small child with her parents in 1853. This was Lotta Crabtree, who became a famous actress known as "The Nation's Darling." The Crabtrees settled in the small foothill mining town of Grass Valley, California, where they ran a boarding house. Beginning at age six, Lotta toured the mining camps, singing, dancing, and playing the banjo. Throughout the 1850s, she entertained in the mining towns in both California and Nevada. Lotta was the Shirley Temple of her day, completely charming every audience who saw her. She eventually formed her own theater company and toured the nation, becoming the highest paid actress of her time. She even inspired dance fads of the 1860s called the "Lotta Polka" and "Lotta Gallup." Though Lotta was extremely famous, she was not notorious like her mentor Lola Montez, who also performed in the mining camps of California, and who is included in this chapter.

Lotta Crabtree (Library of Congress)

San Francisco, which was where most people entered California, gradually became the cultural center of the West, boasting world-class theater, dance, opera, and music. By the latter part of the nineteenth century, San Francisco had become an important destination city for performing acts touring the United States, including those from abroad. By this time, the major city of Southern California, Los Angeles, had also grown to the point of providing another destination for visiting performers. Once the mining booms of the California Mother Lode and the Nevada Comstock Lode were over and the railroad linked California with the rest of the country, Los Angeles overtook San Francisco as California's center of performing arts, eventually becoming home to an entire new industry of show business, movies.

Ah, but that's another story. Before movies were conceived of, acting took place on stages with live performers and a live audience. The vast majority of those performers who strutted upon the stages of history have been utterly forgotten. But the three performers featured here were renowned in their time and live on in legend and lore. In fact, two of the three have even been the subject of feature films. All three of them were not just entertainers, however, but were also notorious for their outrageous behavior. We remember them as much for the flavor of their lives as for their contribution to the arts.

VII. PERFORMERS

LOLA MONTEZ (1821 - 1861)
"The Most Scandalous Woman in the World"

**Lola Montez by Joseph Karl Stieler for
Ludwig of Bavaria, 1847**

Lola Montez, sometimes sarcastically called "The Queen of Bavaria," was also called many more vicious appellations in her lifetime. Like the other women in this book, she made her mark by being bold and pursuing her own unique course in life, pushing convention aside. She became a world famous dancer despite widespread agreement that she was not an exceptional talent in that art. Her notoriety derived mainly from two sources, her violent, audacious temperament and her affair with King Ludwig I of Bavaria. Her relationship with the king propelled her into an international spotlight. She was able to use this notoriety to great advantage, using it to bolster her career. But it wasn't just because of old Ludwig that Lola became successful on stage. Despite any drawbacks in artistry, Lola had a style and a look that drew people in. Getting her name in the news definitely helped attract audiences, but once they were there, it was Lola herself who kept them coming.

Though she performed a wide variety of dances and appeared as an actress in dozens of dramatic and comedic plays, Lola Montez is best known today, as she was during her lifetime, for her Spider Dance. The Spider Dance was based on the popular folk dances of Italy and Spain in which the dancer's moves suggest being attacked by spiders and subsequently vanquishing them. But Lola's version of the dance was creative, sexy, somber, and unlike anything that had been seen before. Without the Spider Dance, Lola's fame would likely have dwindled a few years after the political intrigue she created in Bavaria. That dance was her passport to lasting fame.

Though the stage persona Lola created for herself was Spanish, she was actually born Elizabeth Rosanna Gilbert on February 17, 1821, in the village of Grange, Sligo County, Ireland. Lola's father was Englishman Edward Gilbert, her mother was Irish Elizabeth Oliver, daughter of Charles Oliver, MP, of Oliver Castle, Limerick.

In 1823 Eliza's family went to India where her father died of cholera. Her mother married Scotsman Lieutenant Patrick Craigie the following year, which marked the end of two year old Eliza's relationship with her mother. She was sent to live with Craigie's father in Montrose, Scotland for a few years. At the age of ten, she was uprooted again and sent to live with Craigie's sister Catherine Rae in Sunderland, England. She took drawing lessons there from J. G. Grant, who, after Lola had made a name for herself, was asked what she'd been like as a child. He described her deep blue eyes, dark but flawless skin, black hair, self-assured comportment, and her petulant disposition. "The violence and obstinacy, indeed, of her temper gave too frequent cause of painful anxiety to her good kind aunt; and I remember, upon one occasion it was necessary, before Eliza could receive her lesson, to release her from solitary durance, in which she had been kept all the previous part of the day for some rebellious outbreak of passion. The door was opened, and out came the incipient Lola Montes, looking like a little tigress just escaped from one den to another!"[48]

Eliza's long-suffering aunt had finally had enough during the girl's teen years, and sent her away to school at Camden Place in Bath where she fit in no better than she had anywhere else.

At the age of 15, Eliza eloped and married Lieutenant Thomas James, and the next year the couple went to India where he served in the East India Company. After less than two years in Indian, in 1840, James shipped his wife back to Britain, saying that her health had suffered after a fall from a horse and he thought she would recover better in Scotland with the Craigies. The marriage had not been going smoothly, and James was glad to have an excuse to take a break from his feisty wife.

Some of James' relatives took passage on the same ship and James himself accompanied his wife a short distance before disembarking, making sure she was comfortable. He wrote to his sister in London, asking her to receive Eliza when she arrived and to ensure she was delivered to the steamer that would take her to Scotland. All in all, her husband did everything he could to keep Eliza well chaperoned. But it didn't take long before all of his efforts were usurped by Eliza herself. She met Captain George Lennox on board the ship and soon began a relationship with him, within sight of her husband's relatives. Various people tried to persuade her to break it off with Lennox, but she declined, saying she would do as she liked. When she arrived in England, she refused to have anything to do with any relatives of her stepfather or husband. Instead, she checked into a London hotel and continued her liaison with Lennox. By then, quite a throng of people had heard of what Mrs. James was up to, and, since she stubbornly refused to cease her wanton behavior, they banned her from their company. After her affair with Lennox ended, she went to Edinburgh, where she stayed with a Craigie relative for a time. In 1842 Thomas James sued for a legal separation on the grounds of adultery, and it was granted.

Meanwhile, Eliza took a trip to Spain in March 1842. There she studied dance and brushed up on her Spanish. About a year later she returned to England with aspirations of a stage career. With the help of Lord Malmesbury, she obtained an engagement in June 1843 at Her Majesty's Theatre, London, as "Lola Montez, the Spanish Dancer." She invented an entire progeny of Spanish forebears, an exiled father, who was a general in the army of Don Carlos, and a childhood in Seville, all of which she punctuated by a pronounced vaguely European accent. She was billed as nineteen year old "Dona Lola Montez of Teatro, Seville," an experienced dancer who was making her first appearance in Britain. The truth of the matter was, twenty-two year old Lola Montez was making her first appearance anywhere, as was Eliza Gilbert.

For a debut, it was a good gig. Lola performed between acts of *The Barber of Seville* before a packed audience containing a long list of nobility. On stage, she appeared enveloped in a black mantilla with an organ accompaniment, then flung off her drapery and revealed a black velvet bodice and skirt with red, yellow and violet accents. She then began to dance "El Olano." Her expression throughout was arrogant and unsmiling, her body language intense. One of the movements in the dance was known as "death to the tarantula." It involved tossing her head back with contempt, placing a foot forward and crushing the imaginary arachnid. She received tumultuous applause, bouquets thrown upon the stage, and rose to clamors for an encore.

The dance was typical of Spanish dances, reported the *Evening Mail*, but in the style there was something entirely different from what the audience had seen before. As a technical dancer, the reviewer stated, Lola Montez would not bear comparison with any one of her countrywomen, "but there was nevertheless a kind of national reality about her which was most impressive and novel. The haughtiness with which she stepped, the slow play of the arms, the air of authority with which she once stopped with the hands resting on the hips—all gave an air of grandeur to the dance."

None but a Spaniard, enthused the *Observer*, could do justice to these Spanish dances. She was striking, alluring, enchanting. It seemed that Eliza had created an extremely believable character in Lola.

Lola's debut was a huge success. However, the year she had spent in London defiantly going about with Captain Lennox would return to haunt her. A man in the audience that night went directly to the press to say that the great Spanish beauty was none other than a local woman known as Mrs. James. The London *Age* published this information and cried "Hoax!" Fearing a scandal, the managers of the theater pulled Lola from the bill after her one and only appearance. She wrote a rebuttal to the paper, insisting that she was indeed from Seville and was a refugee from Spain due to political upheaval there. She also threatened to sue.

Despite the setback, Lola persisted in her dancing career and by July had engaged another show, turning the earlier hubbub to her advantage by billing herself as, "Lola Montez, who created so great a sensation at Her Majesty's Theatre." Shortly thereafter she left England for Europe. In Germany she was a hit, but in Berlin she got into trouble for hitting a policeman with her riding whip and for tearing up the court summons that followed. She was released and asked to leave the country. She went on to Poland where her act was not much appreciated. Even less appreciated was her response to the boos of the audience. She made gestures said to be an affront to feminine decency. She was then invited to leave Warsaw, which prompted her to attack the policeman who delivered the message. Lola received a military escort out of Poland. If she was trying to get noticed, she was succeeding. Perhaps it wasn't planned. Perhaps she wasn't that cunning, but her temper was rapidly making her reputation.

Now a year into her professional career, Lola met the composer Franz Listz at one of her performances and the two began a romance. He took her to Paris and introduced her to luminaries of the artistic world, including George Sand, Alexandre Dumas, Victor Hugo, Honoré de Balzac, and others. With the support of these connections, Lola's star began to rise.

In 1845 she fell in love with Frenchman Henri Dujarier, the literary editor of the successful newspaper *La Presse*, but the affair was cut short by tragedy. Over a gambling debt, fellow journalist Jean-Baptiste Rosemond de Beauvallon challenged Dujarier to a duel, which took place March 11. Dujarier chose pistols, but was such a bad shot that he missed de Beauvallon altogether. His opponent's bullet struck its target and Dujarier was killed. Lola was heartbroken and maintained throughout her life that he had been her one great love. Never one to exhibit tact, Lola appeared at the subsequent trial in mourning, as if she were a widow, scandalizing the proceedings. Dujarier left her 18 shares of Palais Royal Theatre in his will. He left everything else to his friend Alexander Dumas.

The following year Lola returned to Munich where she embarked on the most notorious episode of her life. King Ludwig I of Bavaria invited her to dance during the Oktoberfest celebrations, and the sixty year old monarch became entranced by her. By November he had given her an allowance, and by December a house and servants. Lola was keenly interested in politics and wasn't the least bit shy about giving advice to a monarch on state matters. She claimed that it was she who persuaded the king to dismiss his cabinet, which she described as corrupt, and which others have described as anti-Lola, and select a new one from the ranks of the middle classes.

Ludwig was already having popularity problems before Lola came on the scene. There was dissatisfaction among the middle class due to high taxes and strict censorship. The people also didn't like his perpetual extra-marital affairs. Lola was merely the latest, and her abrasive personality made her even more objectionable than some of his other women. Once when Ludwig appeared in his theater box with, not Lola as usual, but his wife Therese, the audience cheered.

After a year, Ludwig made Lola the Countess of Landsfeldt, and at her insistence, began to lobby for her naturalization. When one of Ludwig's ministers advised him to send her away, the minister was fired. Ludwig ignored appeals from Queen Therese, the archbishop, and various government ministers. He was told that his dotage on Lola could incite a revolution, but he clung to the bewitching woman despite all protestations and warnings. Other officials tried to appeal to Lola herself, telling her that her presence was harming the king and the country, causing unrest and controversy. They asked her to leave, even tried to bribe her to do so. She refused.

The country was in an uproar with everybody taking sides. The university students as well divided into two camps, for and against the king's mistress. They rioted in November 1847 and Ludwig ordered the university closed for a year, which only caused further dissent.

In March 1848 there was extensive rioting in the streets and calls for both Lola and Ludwig to leave the country. Lola fell into the hands of rioters, who threw her against a wall and mauled her. She was rescued by the police and brought to the palace. There ensued a clash between the students and the police. Ludwig himself was pelted with stones. In an episode ripe for historical drama, Lola made a desperate escape to Switzerland dressed as a man while the people broke into her house and ransacked it. Ludwig abdicated the throne and, among other concessions, signed an order that if Lola Montez should return to the country, she would be arrested. His son Maximillian II became king.

During the months that followed, Lola occupied a chateau on Lake Geneva waiting to be joined by Ludwig, who never arrived. In November she gave up on the vanquished king and returned to London with a new and not unwelcome cachet. Her engagement in London was a huge success, if not for her dancing and singing abilities, then for her notoriety as the woman who had toppled a king.

In August 1849 Lola married an heir to a fortune, twenty-one year old George Trafford Heald, an English cavalry officer. Because of her notorious immorality, his family was outraged and went out of their way to discredit the woman and find a way to force an annulment. Their efforts paid off when they discovered her first marriage. Since Thomas James and Lola had been legally separated but never officially divorced, the Heald family jumped on this indiscretion and accused Lola of bigamy. She and Heald fled to France and bought a lovely flat where Lola set up a salon like those she had been introduced to when she had earlier come to Paris with Franz Listz. This wasn't the life for young George, and the marriage began to deteriorate.

While Lola was busy entertaining the artistic elite of Paris, the California Gold Rush was drawing in thousands from around the world, and in Paris, mining interests were being sold to anyone with a few francs to invest. Lola was swept up in the excitement and purchased stock in the Eureka mine in Grass Valley. She'd never heard of either the mine or the town, but her blind investment actually worked out. She soon began to receive dividends from the mine.

In 1851, when Lola was thirty, theatrical agent Edward Willis came to Paris and talked Lola into doing a tour of the United States. Her husband George Heald stayed behind. He ended up drowning in a boating accident some months later in Lisbon. And as it happened, Thomas James died of natural causes, leaving Lola twice widowed and single again.

Willis was a savvy promoter. He was able to drum up big audiences for Lola, surrounding her with a crew of excellent actors and dancers, many more technically skilled than she was, and keeping a steady stream of press releases in the papers. He knew that he had a personality on his hands, but may not have known quite how much of one until they were on the road and Lola let her true colors show. She was moody, demanding, and sometimes violent. There were several incidents where she hit a man with her fist or another object, and at least one occasion where she beat her maid. She expected special treatment at every turn, refusing to eat in dining rooms, for instance, with people of lesser stature, and demanding her meals be delivered to her room. When she was provoked, she swore with all the letters of the alphabet like a sailor. But Willis and everybody else in the crew did what

VII. PERFORMERS

they could to make her happy because she was their golden goose.

Lola Montez, 1851

For her debut at the Broadway Theater in New York in December 1851, the house was sold out far in advance, though ticket prices were highly inflated for her appearance. Americans couldn't wait to see her. At least the male Americans couldn't wait. As a woman who had sullied herself by having non-marital sexual relations, she was considered too indecent a person for respectable women to associate with. She was, in fact, barred from staying at many of the best hotels for the same reason. Before her first show, she lived cloistered in a private home and refused to see anyone or give interviews, merely heightening the already feverish desire for a glimpse of the infamous Lola Montez.

The first week of her appearance, the theater made more money than it had ever made in its history. According to reviews, Lola was a competent, but not accomplished dancer, much as had been the evaluation in Europe.

Her next stop was Washington, D.C., where she was billed in the *Daily American Telegraph* (February 9, 1852) as "the Countess of Lansfeldt, the enigma of the 19th century; the dancing girl of Bavaria; the female politician and knight; the greatest wit, beauty, and celebrity of Europe…"

She performed almost daily up and down the Eastern seaboard, and when she returned to New York City in May 1852 she performed her new autobiographical play, "Lola Montez in Bavaria" for the first time. The play covered five periods of her life—the dancer, politician, countess, revolutionist and fugitive. It made her out to be an exiled heroine who had done everything in her power to help the king unite his country. The play got some good reviews from the same reviewers who had loved Lola's dancing. But it got panned terribly by others, especially the Washington D.C. *Daily American Telegraph*: "Lola knows less about acting than she does even about dancing, and she has a voice very like that of a parakeet, or a Guinea fowl, though rather more discordant and sharp. Lola, as an actress, in long petticoats, is a very decided bore. She does not know how to dance; she does not know how to act; she has a horrid voice, bad bust, bad shoulders, bad temper, faded face, and her play don't take." And yet the audiences kept turning up.

When Lola performed her spider dance during her American tour, it usually got special attention, not necessarily in a good way. When she did it in Hartford, Connecticut, the response from the Hartford *Times* was, "she flounces about like a stuck pig, and clenches her short clothes, raising them nearly to her waist, while with her thin, scrawny legs she keeps up a constant thumping upon the stage, as if she was in a slight spasm." Nevertheless, the spider dance was her signature piece, it paid the bills, and it entertained more often than not. It was fun and erotic, but certainly not obscene. The dance itself may not have been the true source of objection. People were predisposed to object to Lola's dancing because they objected to her past. In print, she was insulted time after time, referred to as "the king of Bavaria's worn out wench," a shameless courtesan, concubine, or prostitute who ate up the hard-earned money of the people of Bavaria for the pleasure of a depraved monarch. There were even editors who refused to put her name in their papers at all. Amid all of this, Lola worked hard, held her head up, and challenged her critics head-on.

Though some women did attend her show, they were taking a bit of a dare, as the usual nose-in-the-air contingent maintained that the "Spider Dance could not be witnessed by a virtuous-minded woman in the presence of the opposite sex, without raising the blush of shame and offended modesty upon her cheek."[49]

With a new manager, J. S. Henning, Lola played across the United States, where she continued to exhibit bad behavior and box office success. In New Orleans, the prompter at the Varieties Theater asked her to stop distracting the audience during another dancer's performance. She flew into a rage, verbally assaulted him, kicked him, and stomped out, cursing all the way. She was arrested for assault and battery, but the charges were dropped when tempers cooled.

In the spring of 1853 Lola sailed for the shining city of the west coast, San Francisco, to begin her California tour. What she discovered when she got to the American outback was that California was nothing like the East Coast. It couldn't even be said to be civilized yet, still in the grip of mining fever with dozens of grimy little towns full of trigger-happy saloon jockeys. Even San Francisco was a pioneer city, gritty, diverse, sometimes lawless. It was a place where court cases were often settled with gunfire. None of this intimidated Lola. On the contrary. She had no trouble fitting right in. She went to the horse races with a revolver on one hip and a "rakish-looking knife" on the other. She smoked Cuban cigars and bet $600 on a mare named "Lola Montez." Her namesake won the race.

In July she married Patrick Purdy Hull at Mission Dolores. Hull was a San Franciscan, heavy drinker, gambler and writer of the *Whig* whom she had met on the ship to California. Her new husband became her new manager. It was still so early in San Francisco history that a healthy percentage of the female population occupied the red light district, and most of the men were either unmarried or had left their wives somewhere more respectable, so Lola was now playing to a coarser audience than she'd ever faced before, one that didn't mind so much about her past bedroom adventures. What they cared about was that she was beautiful, showed a lot of flesh and had suggestive moves that sent women-hungry men into spasms of delight. At the end of her act she would slide a silk garter from her leg and toss it into the crowd where a scramble would ensue for the prize. This was the audience Lola was made for, and this was only the beginning. Her show was extended twice in San Francisco, where she played the American Theater and threw a number of benefits for the Fire Department. She then went to Sacramento with similar success.

Having hit the big towns of Northern California, Lola toured the smaller ones in the mining districts of Marysville, Grass Valley, Nevada City, and Downieville, traveling on bumpy dirt roads and living without her usual luxuries. For a woman accustomed to the finest, one who had always demanded the finest, in fact, this seemed out of character. But Lola found that she loved the rugged beauty of California and the appreciative people she encountered along the way.

Over the years, her few thousand franc investment in the Eureka Mine had been paid back several times, and she was delighted to finally see it in person when she came to play in Grass Valley. Lola charmed the citizenry of that small town, but the town charmed her even more. It seemed as if she had finally made it to where she was going, where she'd been destined to end up. At that time, Grass Valley was a fledgling

VII. PERFORMERS

town on the slopes of the Sierra foothills that had only gotten a post office a year before. It was inhabited by Cornish miners who came to work the Empire Mine, one of the richest mines in California. But unlike many of the mining camps in the area, this one was more of a real town, as the miners had brought their families, built houses, churches, gardens, and created a lovely hamlet. The surrounding hills were covered with evergreens and flowing creeks, wildflowers and abundant wildlife.

Surprising everybody, including her new husband, impetuous Lola announced that she was going to live in Grass Valley permanently. In August 1852 she bought a vine-covered white clapboard cottage on Mill Road. She began a costly renovation of the cottage while she and her husband argued about their future. He had no intention of settling down behind the white picket fence in the lazy town of Grass Valley. It sounded more like a cemetery than a town to him. But Lola couldn't be persuaded. She moved into the cottage with her dog Gipsey, as well as her monkey, parrot, canaries, and a grizzly bear cub that she kept in the yard until it bit her and she put it up for sale. In less than two months of landing in Grass Valley, Lola sent Hull packing and filed for divorce.

Lola Montez lived on Mill Road for three years, settled in a way she had never been before. She spent her days hiking or riding her horse through the hills, enjoying nature. She reported that through these walks she was able to communicate spiritually with the love of her life, Henri Dujarier. At home she chain-smoked her way through the day and entertained any persons of note passing through town. One day she went to a mine to learn how to operate a mining cradle. "I've never yet had use for a cradle," she joked, "thank heaven! and my lucky stars!"[50]

Though Grass Valley was a small town, Lola's cottage was on the main road between Oroville and Marysville, a busy route in those days, so plenty of people passed through, and she managed to maintain a healthy social life. But compared to her earlier life, her habits in Grass Valley were extremely sedate.

At times when Lola entertained a large group in her home, she hired neighbor Mary Ann Crabtree, a boarding house owner, to cater the meal. Mrs. Crabtree, a cultured Englishwoman, had a precocious red-headed daughter named Lotta. Lola befriended the girl and taught her to act and dance, never imagining that Lotta Crabtree would one day be the most famous actress of her time.

Life in the foothills wasn't completely without excitement. One late morning in November 1854 Lola burst out of her house with a riding crop in one hand and the local paper, the *Telegraph*, in the other. She ran to the Golden Gate Saloon with a crowd in her wake. She strode up to Mr. Shipley, the paper's editor, and swung her crop at him several times. He caught the whip in his hand and disarmed her. She then cursed him and appealed to the miners around about to come to her defense, but nobody other than Lola was taking the problem seriously. The problem was that the *Telegraph* had reprinted an article from the New York *Times* that spoke of the "Lola Montez-like insolence and effrontery of the Queen of Spain."

Lola's retreat to the rural life was intended to be a retirement, but she was nearly out of money. Though she made a lot of money when she was working, she didn't manage to save much. Out of necessity, she realized the time had come to go back to work.

She put on a few shows in San Francisco, but the crowds didn't show up like they had in the past. Her manager during this time was young Augustus Noel Follin, also her latest lover. He was married with two children, and had left his family in New York while trying to advance his lot in California like so many other young men. Believing that the local scene was tapped out, he suggested taking their show to a real outback—Australia.

In June 1855 thirty-four year old Lola and her crew set sail for Sydney. She played to packed audiences and glowing reviews. When she went on to Melbourne, she met more criticism, one paper going so far as to call the Spider Dance a "subversion of all ideas of public morality." Some towns banned the dance altogether. On the whole, the tour did little more than break even.

In August 1856, over a year after leaving, Lola returned to California with a large white cockatoo as a new pet. On the passage home, Follin jumped or fell overboard and drowned, leaving Lola devastated. It was speculated that he jumped over after they had quarreled or that he had fallen while intoxicated, but Lola had nothing to say about the incident and no one else was present, so the circumstances of Follin's death remain a mystery. Once home, she auctioned off a huge lot of her diamond jewelry, billed as her entire collection, for the benefit of Follin's two children and his widow Caroline. The auction produced almost $10,000.

During the fall of 1856, as Lola performed almost nightly in northern California, she announced that she would be retiring from the stage after this run because she intended to lead a more spiritual life. She sold her Grass Valley property and all the furnishings, then got an apartment in San Francisco where she held séances, all the rage at the time, with her friends.

Before the year was out, though, she was on the road again. She traveled to the "United States." Yes, California really was that foreign! In New York, she made sure that Follin's children were doing okay and there discovered Follin's beautiful younger sister Miriam. She took the twenty year old under her wing, teaching her the stage arts and managing her under the name Minnie Montez. Although Minnie Montez never amounted to much on stage, she became a notorious character in her own right, and rich to boot. She married the founder of a publishing empire, Frank Leslie of *Frank Leslie's Illustrated Newspaper* fame.

Lola began a new tour up and down the Eastern seaboard, again in need of money. She continued to make the usual headlines for her rude and self-important behavior. On a train from Rochester to Buffalo, she sat on a trunk in the baggage car and lit a cigarette. When she was told by the baggage master and then by the train conductor that she was not allowed to ride in the baggage car, she told him that she had traveled the world over and would ride in whatever car she pleased, and that she had "horse-whipped bigger men than he." Then she lit another cigarette and pronounced, "I am going to ride this car to Buffalo." So she did.

In July Lola danced her Spider Dance for the last time. She was getting older, in her mid-thirties, and the demands of dancing were overwhelming her. In the fall of 1857 she began a new career on stage. She delivered a series of lectures, her subjects being "Beautiful Women," "Gallantry," and "The Democracies of Europe," in which she drew upon her extensive travels to compare customs and values in different cultures. Her lectures were witty and intelligent and were attended by women as well as men. She worked as hard at this occupation as she had at the other, appearing almost daily in one town or another.

Next she decided to visit Ireland, the land of her birth, to reconnect with some of the family. While there, she lectured about the differences between Americans and the British. She went on to lecture in Scotland and England, culminating her tour in London.

It was now mid-1859 and Lola was not well. Like many who become aware of their mortality, Lola turned toward religion. She became good friends with former actress Laura Bell, who had also been reborn and was in large part responsible for converting Lola. The two of them could be seen riding through the streets of London in a chariot behind four milk white horses to attend the Methodist church.

In October Lola returned to the United States and settled in Brooklyn, New York, then conducted a series of lectures through the early part of 1860, her topics now leaning towards righteousness. In June she had a stroke that paralyzed her left side and face, leaving her unable to speak clearly and ending her public speaking career. Lola hired a nurse, updated her will and took the name Fanny Gibbons to avoid publicity. Her mother, who had sent her away at such a young age, came to New York for a brief visit after their long separation, but they found they had little to say to one another. The attending doctor described the visits as formal and Mrs. Craigie as cold and distant.

By the end of 1860 Lola had partially recovered from the stroke and was able to walk unaided. During this time, she came into contact with an old school friend from Montrose, Scotland, Maria Buchanan, whom she had not seen since school days. Mrs. Buchanan took pity on her and took her into her home to care for her. Lola's health rapidly deteriorated from the effects of tuberculosis. She was given to fits of coughing that quaked through her weakening body.

Lola Montez died on January 17, 1861, at the age of 39. The official cause of death was pneumonia. Out of a total estate of $1,247, she left $300 to the Magdalene Asylum, a Catholic run institution for unwed mothers, and the rest to Mrs. Buchanan, who used it to pay for the doctor, burial plot, and other expenses. There was no mention of any family members in Lola's will. Mrs. Buchanan wrote a letter to Ludwig I informing him of Lola's death and telling him how glowingly Lola had spoken of his kindness. She did not receive a reply.

Lola Montez was buried in Green-Wood Cemetery in Brooklyn, New York. The Grass Valley house in which she had lived was restored and became a California State Historic Landmark. Lola Montez inspired numerous movie versions of her life and innumerable characters in literature, music, and poetry.

Toward the end of her life she remarked, "I was always notorious, never famous." A good case could be made for that observation. Whether or not she was famous, she was famously interesting and a character who seized the attention of the entire Western world.

DOLLY ADAMS (1860 – 1888)
"The Water Queen"

Dolly Adams

Although Dolly Adams was one of San Francisco's many prostitutes in the 1880s, she had another claim to fame that overshadowed that one. She was an accomplished and widely known aquatic performer during a time when young women performing in large fish tanks was all the rage. Before water

VII. PERFORMERS

ballet, before synchronized swimming, before Esther Williams, there were the "mermaids" of the Gilded Age, swimming in tanks, often with mermaid tails, in front of grand openings, in aquarium displays, and even on stage as the main attraction.

Dolly was by no means the only "Water Queen" in California during that time, but she was the most risqué. Never shy about showing off her voluptuous body, she wore semi-transparent skintight costumes for her shows. She could hold her breath for three minutes underwater in a massive fish tank, and as she did so, she went through the motions of eating, drinking, smoking, sewing, and various other mundane tasks. Then, to the delight of many audience members, particularly the male ones, she got out of the tank dripping wet, leaving little to the imagination, and took a bow.

Dolly Adams was born Ellen Loretta Callahan in 1860, one of several daughters of New Yorkers Patrick and Catherine, both of whom were born in Ireland. Patrick Callahan was a longshoreman and died when Ellen was young, leaving her mother to raise the large brood alone. A strong-willed and beautiful girl, Ellen became a prostitute at the age of sixteen, working in a New York parlor house. Two years later, she was persuaded to go to San Francisco with Madam "Diamond" Carrie Maclay to work in a high-class brothel on Post Street. Now eighteen, Dolly was popular with the clientele and attracted numerous admirers who showered her with gifts. She had beautiful teeth, perfect skin, and tumults of light brown hair down to her knees.

Dolly was an excellent swimmer and swam in the San Francisco Bay. She took lessons from Joseph Fleming in North Beach to learn difficult underwater maneuvers. From there she developed her underwater act, which she performed at the Bella Union and Alhambra theaters either in a tight tank suit or with a mermaid's tail. The act was a huge success and Dolly gave up the prostitution business and toured around the west briefly. Her marketing campaign included a flood of cabinet card photographs that were distributed across the country, and are largely responsible for keeping Dolly's story alive into the twenty-first century. Cabinet cards were 4x6 photographs that first appeared in the 1860s and became a popular format for both family photos and celebrity publicity pictures. The photos in this chapter are from these vintage cards.

During her appearance in Tombstone, Arizona, legend has it that a deadly gunfight erupted during her performance at the famous Bird Cage Theater. That night, as usual, the Earp clan sat on one side of the theater and their foes, the cattle rustling Behans, sat on the other. Normally, if one side cheered the act, the other side booed it, and it wasn't unusual for bullets to fly. But this occasion was more memorable than most. The theater was packed owing to the reputation of the star performer. Shortly after she took the stage to sing, the booing, cheering and arguing began, followed on by gun shots. The battle that took place in the Bird Cage that night left twelve men dead and seven more wounded.

In 1879 Dolly made a huge splash when she donned an elaborate Cupid costume and attended the annual Policeman's Ball in San Francisco. "Dolly was there with her perfect shape fully disclosed in the character of Cupid," reported the *Examiner*. "She was dressed with wings, and carried a bow and a quiver of arrows. Though most of the arrows she shot not from the bow but from her lustrous eyes and each was a dead center shot, hitting alike the youths and bald heads who surrounded her *en masse*."[51] Also in attendance was former president Ulysses S. Grant who marched into the ball with a procession of distinguished guests. Dolly ran up to him arrayed in her beguiling costume and pinned a lily to his lapel. Witnesses recounted that the indomitable Grant "wilted like a wet dishcloth." Best costume prize went to Dolly.

With the money she was raking in, Dolly bought jewelry, mainly diamonds, and fed her opium addiction. After a few years, she gave up her water act. Although she was no longer working in a brothel, she employed herself in the early 1880s by being the mistress of one prominent San Francisco citizen after another. She then moved to New York and bought a boarding house in Manhattan, in a vice-ridden area of the city nicknamed "Satan's Circus" by reformers. Most of the boarders at Dolly's house were theatrical people, and alcohol and drugs continued to be a big part of her life. This lifestyle left her broke and sickly by 1886 when she moved into a cheap apartment at the miserable Oriental Hotel. There among the broken down furniture she prominently displayed photos of herself from her Water Queen days in San Francisco.

Just a couple of months later she became seriously ill with bronchitis and pneumonia. Newspapers on both coasts reported that she was near death and could not possibly recover. As Dolly drifted in and out of consciousness, her mother, eight of her sisters and assorted brothers-in-law crowded into the room, hovered over her death bed, and waited for her to die. "Mrs. Callahan could not keep silence, she lamented the fact that Dolly was caught in 'such a place' and filled the air with protestations of all she wanted to do for her. She grumbled because she had to pay a dollar for 'such a bit of a bottle of medicine as that.' She talked about Dolly's death until the sufferer cried out with horror and visitors in the room begged her to hold her tongue. 'I have done all I could for Dolly,' said Mrs. Callahan. 'I'm not a pauper, God knows. I've got a pretty bit of money and I'm paying for all this. If Dolly dies I'll give her a first-class funeral, be sure of that.'"[52]

Finally, the family was persuaded to send Dolly to a hospital where she got better care and recovered. She then returned to San Francisco. When her old friend and madam Carrie Maclay saw her again she was shocked to see the young woman so haggard and sickly. Maclay herself died several years later from addictive opium use.

There is a popular legend surrounding Dolly's final years. It is said that she met a wealthy Chinese businessman on a trip to California. He fell in love with her and wanted her to return to Peking with him. She said she would go only as his wife, so they were married and off she went. She made him promise that if she should die in China, he would return her body to San Francisco.

A few years later, in 1888, the steamer the *City of New York* arrived in San Francisco Bay with an elaborate Chinese coffin aboard. It contained the body of Dolly Adams, who had died in China and been returned as promised.

Dolly Adams Cabinet Card

The actual facts surrounding her death are less romantic. On a several weeks tour of the Orient, she learned of her mother's death and booked passage on the *City of New York*, sailing for San Francisco with the intent of going on to visit her family. Diminished by the effects of syphilis and opium addiction, she contracted pneumonia on board and died. Her body was embalmed aboard ship and she was buried in San Francisco upon arrival. Her few remaining possessions consisted of clothing and a tin trunk which contained some money, a railroad bond worth $1,000, some jewelry and several fans, altogether worth about as much as the estate lawyer spent to settle her affairs.

Dolly Adams was only 27 when she died and would likely have faded from public consciousness soon after if not for the many cabinet card photographs she posed for in her heyday. Her image can still be purchased and admired today, mementos of one of the more unusual fads in the entertainment world.

ISADORA DUNCAN (1877 – 1927)
"The Mother of Modern Dance"

Isadora Duncan

Isadora Duncan is most famously known, even by those who know nothing else about her, for the horrific way in which she died. On September 14, 1927, she dined with friends, including her long time intimate, Mary Desti, who presented her with a gift of a dramatically long, colorful scarf. After dinner, Isadora wrapped one end of the scarf around her neck and climbed into an open car. She waved farewell as her beau drove the car away. The trailing end of the scarf fluttered in the breeze, then wrapped itself around the rear axle and yanked Isadora out of her seat. She was dashed to the road, fatally breaking her neck.

Isadora Duncan's notorious death at the age of fifty was only the last of many shocking events in her life. She was a world-famous dancer who is credited with inventing modern dance. She was also a feminist, a Communist, an atheist, and an advocate of free love, none of which were considered acceptable to Americans in general at the time.

Angela Isadora Duncan was born in San Francisco on May 26, 1877, the youngest of four children of banker and mining engineer Joseph Charles Duncan and Mary Isadora Gray Duncan. Shortly after Isadora's birth, her father got into hot water for issuing fraudulent stock certificates. His trials lasted until 1882. He spent most of that time in the county jail, unable to make bail. The end result was that, after several years in jail, he walked free. Isadora was then five years old, but by then, her parents had divorced. Mary Duncan moved the family across the bay to Oakland, where she worked as a seamstress and piano teacher, barely getting by.

Both of Isadora's parents were aficionados of the arts, so she grew up in an atmosphere replete with music, literature, and dance. She was in love with dance from an early age, and took dance lessons after school, but she preferred her own freeform movements to traditional ballet. She was well equipped for her art, being tall, beautiful, and graceful. At the age of ten, she dropped out of school, finding it stifling, but she continued to study dance and read literary classics. She gave dancing lessons to local children to make extra money for the family.

When she was 19 Isadora went to Chicago and joined Augustin Daly's theater company. She appeared in a vaudeville show as "The California Faun" at the Masonic Temple Roof Garden. During the performance, she floated

VII. PERFORMERS

about to Mendelssohn's "Spring Song." She then went to New York and continued her studies in theater and dance.

Her entire family ended up in New York, performing as a group in private drawing rooms and at garden parties. Her mother played the piano and her sister recited poetry. Her brother Raymond was the choreographer. The troupe became a popular novelty act for the wealthy.

It was during this time that Isadora developed her personal style of movement. At that time, dance in the Western world meant primarily classical ballet, and Isadora's art was a clear rejection of ballet with its pointe shoes and tight-fitting costumes. She performed in loose, filmy garments, barefoot. Nobody had ever danced on stage in bare feet, at least not for nearly two thousand years. Isadora took her inspiration from the classical Greeks, from the figures on their pottery, their statues, and their philosophy, with an emphasis on being as natural as possible. Today, the style of dance she invented is called "free dance," a term she would likely approve. Freedom was always the major emphasis of her style.

Isadora slowly began to get theater engagements, taking her parlor act on stage. Not everyone was enthusiastic. Another San Francisco dancer, Lola Yberri, saw one of Isadora's performances in New York at the Lyceum Theater. She termed it a "disaster." "Miss Duncan doesn't dance at all; she just poses. She posed in Grecian costumes while Justin Huntley McCarthy recited the poetry of the Persian Omar Khayyam. The critics said it was awful and that Miss Duncan looked as if she were in swaddling clothes and in danger of losing them at any moment."[53]

After scraping together enough money to take passage on a cattle ship, the family moved to London in 1898 and continued to perform in private homes. Isadora next went to Paris, where she began to attract the right kind of attention.

A big boost to her career came in 1902 in Budapest, where she was a resounding success and ran sold out for thirty days.

In one memorable 1903 performance, given privately to seventy-five prominent sculptors, painters, musicians, and critics in Berlin, she interpreted classical and renaissance paintings through dance. In Vienna, she danced for Emperor Francis Joseph at his villa. He was enthralled. The same thing happened when she went to Berlin and performed for Kaiser Wilhelm. The two heads of state them found themselves vying for the dancer to take up residence in their cities. Both offers were fabulous for Isadora's career. What tipped the scale was that the female art patrons of Berlin told her they would build her her own theater. The Berliners raised $250,000 to build a classically styled theater that Isadora could call her home. A sculptor was commissioned to create a life-sized statue of her for the grand entrance. Among the monetary contributors was Countess Maria von Bülow, the wife of the Chancellor of Germany.

Isadora realized one of her earliest dreams when she finally went to Athens to study Greek art. While there, she wore an ancient Greek style gown and went barefoot in the streets, much as she did when on stage interpreting the classics. Needless to say, she got noticed, but she didn't do it for publicity. She did it to put herself into the proper frame of mind for her studies. She wasn't alone in her obsession with ancient Greece. She came by it naturally. "In fact," pointed out a reporter for the Stockton *Independent*, "the whole Duncan family have studied ancient Greece and its customs to such an extent that they are now a bit weird to have about the house. It is said that Miss Duncan's brother insists on emptying half a glass of wine on the floor, whenever one is given him, as a libation to the Olympian gods." Raymond Duncan married an Athenian and nicknamed her Penelope, and continued for years to live according to Greek customs and philosophies. Upon returning from an extended trip to Greece in 1909, he, his wife, and their son Memalkus created a commotion when they disembarked in New York in a freezing gale wearing armless Greek tunics with bare legs and sandals.

In 1904, the building completed, Isadora opened her dance school in Grunewald, Germany, where her sister Elizabeth served as her assistant. Her most passionate pupils—Anna, Maria-Theresa, Irma, Liesel, Gretel, and Erika—called themselves the "Isadorables." The girls lived at the school,

VII. PERFORMERS

clad in the same dancing costume as their teacher amid statues and vases in a building resembling a Greek temple.

In 1905, approaching thirty, Isadora had a relationship with Gordon Craig, a theater set designer and the son of famous actress Ellen Terry. The affair produced a daughter, Deirdre Beatrice, born in 1906. Although Craig remained Isadora's friend for life, the romantic relationship was short-lived.

As her fame grew, the pressure on Isadora to perform in America also grew. She was reluctant to do so because she found American audiences generally lacking education and familiarity with dance. But she was persuaded to come back in 1908 for the purpose of establishing another dancing school. She appeared in a two-hour, one-woman show at the Criterion Theater in New York, in which she danced on stage in a flowing gown with bare legs and arms and interpreted several pieces of classical music. After her first run, it seemed she had been right to doubt the sophistication of American audiences, but when she appeared later in the year at the Metropolitan opera house, the place was packed to overflowing and the reception was wildly enthusiastic. American women, especially, may have been more ready for Isadora's style than she could have imagined. There were those who saw her as the leader of an insurrection, someone who would emancipate women from a life of convention and painful corsets to a natural state of free womanhood. Isadora's dancing spoke to a growing number of women who demanded equality, freedom, and, of course, the right to vote.

By now Isadora was an international phenomenon with numerous admirers and imitators. She was feted by dancers, painters, writers, and

Isadora Duncan
(Photo by Arnold Genthe)

especially sculptors, perhaps because of her likeness to a classical statue when she performed. The sculptor Laredo Taft said of her, "Poetry personified. She is not the tenth Muse, but is all nine Muses in one." Emile-Antoine Bourdelle, who created sculptures for the Théâtre des Champs-Élysées, built in 1913, said that Isadora Duncan was his primary inspiration, and included her image on the façade and on the murals in the auditorium.

Artistic dance enjoyed a new wave of popularity in the United States in the 1910s, and Isadora was largely responsible for this. Across the country, women got together in their drawing rooms and performed dances similar to hers for one another's appreciation. They also filled the theaters when such dancers came to perform, supporting the careers of many young women who followed in the footsteps of Isadora.

Isadora's second child, Patrick Augustus, was born in 1910. His father was Paris Singer, the son of sewing machine magnate Isaac Singer. Singer helped Isadora establish her second dancing school in Paris. It was during this period, when Isadora and her mother resided in Bellevue, Paris, that Isadora met her lifelong friend Mary Dempsey, who had renamed herself Mary Desti. Desti had fled the U.S. after a failed marriage, arriving in Paris with no money and no prospects. On her first day there, she met Isadora's mother, who invited her home. She too had a young son, Preston Sturges (who became a famous writer and director of Hollywood movies). Desti and Isadora were soon inseparable. At times, Desti's bond with Isadora was greater even than her devotion to her son, who was often left with others while Desti and Isadora travelled together.

In a horrible tragedy in 1913 both of Isadora's young children were drowned. In the care of a nanny, their car went through the railing of a bridge and plunged into the River Seine. By the time the car was pulled out with a crane, the nanny and the two children were dead inside. The world was shocked by the accident, and people came by Isadora's house to leave white flowers, covering the entire grounds. Isadora was devastated and announced that she would never again dance on stage. In her autobiography, she says she begged a

VII. PERFORMERS

young Italian sculptor, Romano Romanelli, to sleep with her because she was desperate for another child. As a result, she gave birth to a son on August 13, 1914, but the child died shortly afterward.

World War I encroached heavily onto Isadora's world around that same time. Her Paris school was turned into a Red Cross hospital and her Neuilly studio became a children's refuge. She herself nursed the wounded in Normandy. Unable to continue teaching her students under those conditions, Isadora returned to the United States and brought several of her pupils with her. She opened a dance school at Gramercy Park in New York. She did not, however, completely forsake Europe. In one notable event, she and her brother took to the streets of Athens to arouse the Greeks to support their prime minister, Eleftherios Venizelos, in his controversial drive to join the Allied forces. Raymond played a hand organ and Isadora danced barefoot from her hotel to Venizelos's home, pausing now and then to sing the national anthem of France, "La Marseillaise."

As the war was in full swing in Europe, the Isadorables, who had been performing in the U.S., began to long for home. Isadora decided to take them back to their parents by way of then neutral Italy. They booked passage on the *Dante Alighieri*, sailing on May 6, 1915. Once everybody was on board and in their cabins, Isadora reappeared on deck to wave goodbye to Desti, her son Preston, and a number of other friends who were gathered at the dock. She was highly emotional, sobbing into her handkerchief. Desti was also in tears. Isadora leaned over the railing, reaching toward her friend. "Mary!" she cried. "If you don't come with me, I don't know what I'll do!" Desti turned to her son and said, "Do the best you can, darling. Keep things going. I'll send you some money as soon as I can!" Desti then hurried up the gangplank with no money and no luggage. She appeared beside Isadora on deck, shivering in the cold night air and waving down at her son. A friend in the crowd sent both his overcoat and a wad of cash aboard for Desti's ticket, and the two friends were off on another adventure.

Isadora was by now so famous that she was referred to as the woman who "revolutionized the entire art of the dance." She had wowed audiences the world over, but even though she was often begged to do so, she had never brought her show to her home town of San Francisco. She was finally talked into it by her manager, Will L. Greenbaum, so at the conclusion of a three-month South American tour, she was scheduled to make her appearance in November 1916 in California. San Franciscans were ecstatic. They snatched up all available tickets.

Shortly before her appearance, Isadora injured her leg and ankle in rehearsal and cancelled her California tour.

The following year, by which time the U.S. had officially joined WWI, the tour was rescheduled and at long last Isadora danced for the hometown crowd, performing with the local symphony orchestra to interpret several pieces of classical music. In each show, she included "La Marseillaise" as well, and the audience always stood during her interpretation of it.

The following year Isadora began a passionate relationship with American poet and playwright Mercedes de Acosta. Acosta was known more for the company she kept than her literary accomplishments. She claimed she could seduce any woman away from any man, and she had dozens of conquests to prove it. Among the legions of her female lovers were Greta Garbo, Marlene Dietrich, and Ona Munson. She could typically be seen on the streets of New York in men's pants, a tricorne hat, and cape, her black hair slicked back with brilliantine. Actress Tallulah Bankhead called her "Countess Dracula." The relationship with Isadora continued on and off for several years.

After the war, the six Isadorables, professionally named the "Isadora Duncan Dancers," returned to the U.S. and successfully toured with classical pianist George Copeland. Isadora formally adopted all of them in 1918.

At the conclusion of WWI, the Russian Revolution took place, putting the Bolsheviks in power and leading to the formation of the Soviet Union. The transformation of Russia from a monarchy to a socialist republic attracted the attention of many artists of the day who believed that the Russians had landed on a form of government that would lead to peace, prosperity, an end to poverty, and freedom of artistic expression. Isadora Duncan was one of these. She embraced Communism and opened a dancing school in Moscow. Toward the end of 1921 she officially moved from Paris to Moscow. "I quit Europe," she said, "where art is crushed by commercialism."[54] She predicted that Russia would end up leading the world toward a spiritual and artistic rebirth. For her part, she believed that the most valuable thing she could do with her life was to teach children to dance and expose them to classical music. "If the crown prince of Germany," she said, "had learned, before his sixth year, to dance to the music of Beethoven's Ninth Symphony, instead of being permitted to play with toy soldiers, the World War might have been averted."[55]

The following year, at the age of 45, she married famous Russian poet Sergei Yesenin, who was only 27 years old. He had a boyishly handsome face and wavy blond hair. Isadora said they had loved one another in a previous life in Egypt where she was a dancing girl and he was a soldier. When she saw him in this life, she said, she recognized him immediately, and knew they were destined to be together.

Isadora Duncan and Sergei Yesenin, 1923

She then went on a tour of Europe and the United States, leaving her Moscow school in the hands of her adopted daughter and Isadorable Irma. When she and Sergei arrived at Ellis Island, they were detained. She was questioned about her politics and her intentions regarding her visit to the country of her birth, for she was now seen as sympathetic to Communist Russia and potentially an agent of the Russian government. She and her husband were finally allowed entry, but Isadora did not confine herself to dancing. She made political statements at her performances, declaring herself "a red," and was openly critical of Americans and American culture. She also wore a scanty costume that many thought inappropriate for the stage. In Boston, her costume kept shifting around, threatening to fall off completely and scandalize decent Bostonians. As it was, the costume was nearly transparent and left nothing to the imagination. The bodice frequently fell open to reveal her naked breasts. The performance caused so many gasps and tense moments that she was banned forever from appearing in Boston again. The same thing happened in Chicago.

One by one, cities and even whole states began to declare themselves off limits to the dancer. In other places where she did dance, certain precautions were taken to insure that she didn't offend anybody. In Indianapolis, four uniformed policemen were placed near the stage with orders to arrest her immediately if she took off too much clothing or began to spout red propaganda. As a result, she changed her program "giving only dances of tragic sorrow and Christian humility, as I deemed any expression of joyousness or freedom under the circumstances [to be] quite impossible."[56]

Isadora claimed that the objections she encountered were purely political, that she had been wearing the same costumes for twenty years and nobody had complained before. Some particularly unkind critics suggested that maybe the complaints were coming because she was twenty years older. She wore loose garments in order to move freely, she explained. Her art was symbolic of the freedom of women, which she acknowledged was frightening and repugnant to many. Art should be viewed in a different light than everyday life, she said. She pointed out that nobody would call the Venus de Milo indecent. Why, then, did they say such things about a dancer's body? She reminded the public that when she had first appeared on stage in bare feet, she was booed and berated, and now all the best dancers shed their shoes.

She had intended to tour the entire country, ending on the West Coast, but after her appearance in Chicago, she was broke and had to borrow money to get back to New York, where she appeared a few more times. She then borrowed money for the passage back to Europe. From the deck of her ship, she fired a broadside at the country of her birth. "I would rather live in Russia on black bread and vodka," she declared, "than in the United States at the best hotels. We have freedom in Russia!"[57] She was particularly critical about prohibition, which did not stop her in the least from drinking, saying that the stuff that passed for liquor in America would kill an elephant, and that if she had stayed longer, it would have killed her as well.

When they reached Paris, Isadora and Sergei checked into the Crillon Hotel where they fell into a drunken brawl during which Sergei threw glasses and anything else he could get his hands on. The manager of the hotel called the police and they took him away for the night, then the couple was asked to leave the hotel. When he was released, Sergei went to Berlin to stay with Maxim Gorky, and Isadora took a break at Versailles. The two divorced in 1924.

A year later Sergei hung himself in the Hotel Angleterre in St. Petersburg, leaving a suicide note written in blood.

Isadora's career began to wane in the late 1920s. She was getting older and her dancing days were numbered. She was still a celebrity, not as much for her art as for her scandalous behavior, which included public drunkenness and numerous lovers of both sexes. She was also out of money and relied on friends to put her up in hotels or rent her apartments as she moved around Europe. Among her friends were F. Scott and Zelda Fitzgerald, who tried to help Isadora write her autobiography, hoping it would sell well enough to support her.

She was disillusioned, depressed, and bored with life. She said as much one evening at a dinner party hosted by Desti in Nice. She said she wanted to die, but couldn't figure out how to pull it off. It was September 14, 1927, and Isadora was fifty years old. Desti presented her with a fine red silk scarf designed by Russian artist Roman Chatov. Wearing the gift, Isadora climbed into an Amilcar CGSS sportscar, race car driver Benoît Falchetto at the wheel. Popular culture claims that as the car started off, Isadora called, *"Adieu, mes amis. Je vais à la gloire!"* (Farewell, my friends, I go to glory.) According to Desti, however, what she actually said was, "Je vais à la'amour" (I am off to love), implying that she and her companion were returning to the hotel for a romantic tryst.

We all know what happened next. Within moments the scarf wrapped around the axle and Isadora Duncan was dead.

When Gertrude Stein heard the news, she famously, and bluntly, quipped, "Affectations can be dangerous."

Isadora was cremated and her ashes were placed next to those of her children in the columbarium at Père Lachaise Cemetery in Paris.

Isadora's autobiography, *My Life*, was published posthumously by Boni and Liveright. In 1929 Mary Desti published another book about her entitled *The Untold Story*, describing the years 1921 through 1927. Isadora's daughter Irma Duncan also wrote a book entitled, *Isadora Duncan's Russian Days and Her Last Years in France*.

Isadora's many protégés continued dancing and teaching her particular style of dance. In addition to her students, there were several other dancers who carried on her work. Among them was Julia Levien who formed the Duncan Dance Guild in the 1950s and the Duncan Centenary Company in 1977. Mignon Garland, a pupil of two of Isadora's key students, formed the Isadora Duncan Heritage Society. Garland was responsible for getting an alley in San Francisco named after her hero. Isadora Duncan Lane is located off of Taylor Street between Geary and Post.

In 1987 Isadora Duncan was inducted into the National Museum of Dance and the Hall of Fame. Her likeness is included in the mural in the entrance to the Monadnock

Building on Market Street in San Francisco along with other notables, including Harvey Milk, Lotta Crabtree, and Mary Ellen "Mammy" Pleasant.

Many movies, books, ballets, stage plays, poems and musical numbers have been created about or have been inspired by Isadora Duncan. Among these, the Sylvia Plath poem *Fever 103* alludes to Isadora's scarves, and the theme song of the TV show *Maude* includes the line, "Isadora was the first bra-burner/Ain't ya glad she showed up?"

Isadora Duncan frequently said that artists are revolutionists. Certainly she was one. She brought about a revolution in the world of dance, creating a new art form. Her influence is easily seen even today, as dance has progressed into post-modernism and contemporary forms that emphasize natural and improvisational movements.

Isadora Duncan

ABOUT THE AUTHOR

Robin C. Johnson is the author of books about California history and natural history, both of which she loves to explore. She was born in Central California where she lives conveniently equidistant from the Pacific Ocean and the Sierra Nevada mountains. Robin is a retired computer software designer devoting her time to travel, writing, theater and any culinary adventures that come her way.

NOTES

[1] Eliza W. Farnham, *California in-doors and out*, New York: Dix, Edwards & CO.,1856. p. 22.

[2] "Mrs. Botkin Talks about J. P. Dunning," *The San Francisco Call*, August 23, 1898, p. 16.

[3] "Mrs. Botkin Talks about J. P. Dunning," *The San Francisco Call*, August 23, 1898, p. 16.

[4] "Mrs. Botkin Under Arrest," *The San Francisco Call*, August 24, 1898, p. 16.

[5] "Takes Fate Calmly," *Sacramento Union*, March 28, 1906, p. 3.

[6] "Mrs. LeDoux Denies Rumors," *Santa Cruz Evening Sentinel*, January 17, 1907, p. 6.

[7] "Emma LeDoux Pleads Guilty," *Amador Ledger*, January 28, 1910, p. 8.

[8] "Trunk Murderess is in San Quentin Cell," *San Francisco Call*, February 3, 1910, p. 1.

[9] Hereford, Robert A., "Old Man River—Famous Woman Gambler," St. Louis *Post-Dispatch*, June 18, 1943, p. 3D.

[10] Watkins, John McLain, "Calamity Jane| A pageant-drama in three acts" (1961). Graduate Student Theses, Dissertations, & Professional Papers. 1730, p. 56.

[11] "Madame Mustache, 'Stem Winder' and Calamity Jane," *Herald-Advance*, July 20, 1906, p. 5.

[12] "The Shadow Woman," *The San Francisco Examiner*, June 13, 1897, p. 6.

[13] "She is the Queen of Pickpockets," *The San Francisco Chronicle*, Oct. 30, 1896, p. 9.

[14] "Duchess Murder Gang Opens Defense as Prosecution Rests," *The Fresno Bee*, May 24, 1940, p. 17.

[15] "Duchess Gets 30-Day Reprieve," *San Pedro News Pilot*, June 20, 1941, p. 9.

[16] "Olson Refuses to Save Duchess," *San Pedro News Pilot*, November 19, 1941, p. 1.

[17] "Amy Crocker Now Buddha Devotee," *Sacramento Union*, Volume 118, Number 110, 13 December 1909, p. 5.

[18] "Unique Bal Masque Held Sunday Night in Gotham" *San Francisco Call*, Volume 105, Number 49, 18 January 1909, p. 2.

[19] "The Price I Paid for My Pearls," *San Diego Union and Daily Bee*, 23 May 1920.

[20] "Aimée Crocker Gouraud's 12th Husband So She Says", *Oakland Tribune*, 17 January 1926.

[21] "I Knew Charley Parkhurst," *Evening Sentinel*, January 31, 1903, p. 2.

[22] "Concerning Cross-Eyed Charley, Female Stage Driver of Santa Cruz," *Evening Sentinel*, January 8, 1903, p. 4.
[23] Otto, Ernest, "Old Santa Cruz," *Santa Cruz Sentinel*, April 11, 1948, p. 11.
[24] Santa Cruz *Sentinel*, October 1, 1880.
[25] "Charley Parkhurst," *Santa Cruz Sentinel*, April 9, 1898, p. 1.
[26] "Seeking Death," *San Francisco Chronicle*, January 31, 1872, p. 3.
[27] W. C. Morrow, "The Story of the Little Frog Catcher," *San Francisco Examiner*, March 27, 1892, p. 19.
[28] "San Francisco Correspondence," *Ventura Signal Supplement*, October 7, 1876, p. 2.
[29] "Forty-Year Masquerade as Man Bared by Death," *San Bernardino Sun*, September 22, 1936, p. 4.
[30] "Law Courts," *Daily Alta California*, November 9, 1851, p. 2.
[31] "Trouble With China," *Daily Alta California*, 14 December 1851, p. 2.
[32] Herb Caen, "That was San Francisco," *The San Francisco Chronicle*, May 26, 1942, p. 11.
[33] "Mooney Accuses Dinan of Receiving Bribes from Evil Resorts," *The San Francisco Call*, June 15, 1907, p. 16.
[34] "Frank Daroux Denies his Wife Gave Him Money," *San Francisco Chronicle*, May 23, 1917, p. 4.
[35] "Social Gossip," *San Francisco Chronicle*, 31 December 1871, p. 8.
[36] W. H. L. Barnes, *Argument for the Defendant, Sarah Althea Sharon vs. William Sharon* (San Francisco: Barry, Baird & Co., 1884), p. 91.
[37] "The Sharon Case," *San Francisco Chronicle*, 25 December 1884, p. 3.
[38] Helen Holdredge Collection, San Francisco Public Library.
[39] Milton S. Gould, *A Cast of Hawks* (La Jolla: Copley Books, 1985), p. 336.
[40] Lewis and Hall, *Bonanza Inn*, pp. 212-214.
[41] "Pauper's Grave Escaped by Sarah Althea Terry," *Oakland Tribune*, 16 February 1937, p. 2.
[42] "Life Story of Mrs. Charley Fair," *Los Angeles Herald*, Volume XXIX, Number 353, 21 September 1902, p. 9.
[43] "Life Story of Mrs. Charley Fair," *Los Angeles Herald*, Volume XXIX, Number 353, 21 September 1902, p. 9.
[44] "If Countess Why Not More?", *The San Francisco Examiner*, April 30, 1893, p. 3.
[45] "An Oregon Countess," *Seattle Post-intelligencer*, April 30, 1893, p. 4.
[46] "The Countess D'Henriot," *Los Angeles Herald*, January 13, 1894, p. 6.

[47] "A Tenderloin Queen," *Washington Evening Times*, August 26, 1898, p. 5.

[48] *Sunderland Herald* 31 August 1849, page 5.

[49] *The Shasta Courier*, July 16, 1853, p. 2.

[50] *Washington Daily Evening Star*, October 22, 1853, p. 1.

[51] *The San Francisco Examiner*, "The Wages of Sin," May 7, 1886, p. 2.

[52] *The San Francisco Examiner*, "The Wages of Sin," May 7, 1886, p. 2.

[53] "Wins Plaudits Far From Home," *San Francisco Call*, February 25, 1903, p. 5.

[54] "Isadora Duncan to Stay in Russia," *Riverside Daily Press*, October 11, 1921, p. 1.

[55] "Secure Peace by Teaching Children Dancing She Says," *San Luis Obispo Daily Telegram*, July 12, 1922, p. 4.

[56] Isadora Duncan Resents Hoosier Ban on Dance, *San Francisco Call*, November 20, 1922, p. 11.

[57] "Famed Dancer Attacks U. S. on Departure," *San Luis Obispo Daily Telegram*, February 3, 1923, p. 1.

www.ingramcontent.com/pod-product-compliance
Lightning Source LLC
Chambersburg PA
CBHW061641040426
42446CB00010B/1519